THE NEW WINDMILL BOOK OF

# Stories from Different Genres

EDITED BY MIKE HAMLIN, CHRISTINE HALL
AND JANE BROWNE

Heinemann
New Windmills

Heinemann is an imprint of Pearson Education Limited,
a company incorporated in England and Wales, having
its registered office at Edinburgh Gate, Harlow, Essex,
CM20 2JE. Registered company number: 872828

Heinemann is a registered trademark of Pearson Education limited.



13

ISBN: 978 0 435124 95 3

Acknowledgements

The editor and publisher would like to thank the following for permission to use copyright material:

Papermac for 'The Superstitious Man's Story' from 'A Few Crusted Characters' in *The Collected Short Stories of Thomas Hardy*, p.3; Richard Dalby for 'The Violet Car' by E. Nesbit, originally published in the collection, *Fear* by E. Nesbit (Stanley Paul, 1910), reprinted in *The Virago Book of Ghost Stories* edited by Richard Dalby (Virago, 1987), p.7; 'Harry' by Rosemary Timperley reproduced by permission of The Agency (London) Ltd. HARRY first published by Pan in *The Third Ghost Book*. All rights reserved and enquiries to The Agency (London) Ltd 24 Pottery Lane, London W11 4LZ fax: 0171 727 9037, p.22; Faber and Faber Ltd for 'Crossing Over' by Catherine Storr, p.32; 'The Man with the Twisted Lip' by Sir Arthur Conan Doyle, copyright 1996 Sheldon Reynolds, Administrator of the Conan Doyle Copyrights. Reproduced by kind permission of Jonathan Clowes Ltd, London, on behalf of Sheldon Reynolds, Administrator of the Conan Doyle Copyrights. p.40; Random House for 'The Lieabout' by Margery Allingham from *The Allingham Case Book*, published by Chatto and Windus, p.66; Richard Curtis Associates Inc for 'Forever After' by Jim Thompson, p.74; The Society of Authors as the Literary Representative of the Estate of Virginia Woolf for 'The Legacy' by Virginia Woolf, p.108; 'Twelve Hours – Narrative and Perspectives' © Adèle Geras 1985. Permission granted by the Author, p.116; A P Watt Ltd on behalf of The Literary Executors of the Estate of H. G. Wells for the extract from 'The Time Machine', p.126; 'The Veldt' by Ray Bradbury reprinted by permission of Don Congdon Associates, Inc. Copyright © 1950 by the Curtis Pub. Co., renewed 1977 by Ray Bradbury, p.138; Random House for 'The Quest For *Blank Claveringi*' from *Eleven* by Patricia Highsmith, published by William Heinemann, p.185; G. K. Sprinkle for 'Serena Sees', p.211.

The Publishers have made every effort to trace the copyright holders, but if they have inadvertently overlooked any, they will be pleased to make the necessary arrangements at the first opportunity.

Cover illustration by James Brace
Cover design by The Point
Typeset by Tek-Art, Croydon, Surrey
Printed in China by CTPS

# Contents

## Horror 163

# Introduction

Genre is about different ways of categorizing writing. Whenever we read a text we immediately begin to sort between categories. Is it fiction or non-fiction? If fiction, is it crime or sci-fi, love or horror? If non-fiction, is it description or argument, explanation or instruction?

As experienced readers we can usually identify quite quickly which genre we are dealing with. We have learned to pick up the subtle clues, codes, conventions, styles and forms which characterize a particular genre.

But does genre matter? It certainly draws attention to the way writing is constructed and the way in which writers target their writing for particular purposes and audiences. Studying genre also enables the reader to understand the mechanics of writing itself, including language, structure and other organizational features.

This collection presents seventeen stimulating and enjoyable stories from five narrative genres – Ghost, Crime, Love, Science Fiction and Horror.

The stories are grouped by genre. Each genre selection:

- has its own general and story-specific introductions;
- opens with a pre-twentieth-century story from one of the authors listed in the National Curriculum;
- contains a selection of stories which exemplify different aspects of the genre under consideration;
- concludes with:
  **a** detailed suggestions for comparative study, as required in the **wider reading** assignments at GCSE and beyond
  **b** a range of opportunities for **original student writing** based on some of the features and insights particular to each genre.

## Section 1
# Ghost

Ghost stories provide us with ways of thinking about death and dying. They help us explore our uncertainties about the supernatural and whether there is any form of life after death. They build upon the fact that, whatever we believe, no one can be definite about what happens to the spirit when our bodies die. All of us will experience a fear of dying and most of us will experience great grief when someone we love dies.

Ghost stories use our fear of death and the unknown to create suspense in the reader. They draw on deep-rooted superstitions and beliefs that perhaps we all have an allotted time to die. They portray the meeting of two worlds – the worlds of the living and the dead – and they create tension about whether a character will step over the borders from one world to the other.

They also draw on our experience of what happens to people who are grieving. When people we love die, grief can make us lose our grip on everyday reality. Life can seem pointless, and we so desperately want to see the person we are missing that it is common to imagine catching sight of the dead person. Ghost stories often keep the reader guessing about whether the characters have actually seen a ghost, or are being driven by grief or fear to imagine that they have.

Most commonly, ghost stories deal with the premature or violent death of the ghost character. They build a story around the idea of an interrupted life, to which the ghost needs to return to tie up the loose ends. Places and times are highly significant in ghost stories. The exact time or place of a person's death can take on a symbolic significance. So can objects, music or perfumes associated with the dead person.

Because ghost stories are hard to believe, writers use devices that make the story seem more authentic. The stories are often told in the first person, to suggest that the writer actually had the experience. Many contain a lot of direct speech, with people apparently telling the story 'in their own words'. The central characters are often sensible, down-to-earth people who would not usually have wild imaginations.

The tension in ghost stories usually builds up as we wait to see whether the world of the dead or the living will win in the end. But because we know that we cannot go on living for ever, we are also aware that any victory for the living characters is only a temporary one. This leaves writers with lots of possibilities for dramatic twists at the ends of their stories.

# The Superstitious Man's Story
## Thomas Hardy

This is from a collection of Hardy's stories called *Life's Little Ironies* which was first published in 1894. *The Superstitious Man's Story* is one of a series of linked tales which are grouped together under the heading *A Few Crusted Characters*.

Hardy has invented a set of neighbours who meet a traveller returning to his father's home in Wessex. On the coach journey the local people tell the traveller stories of the 'crusted characters' to bring him up-to-date with the news. Each of the nine tales is told in direct speech by one of the Wessex people, and there are short linking conversations between the stories.

**Thomas Hardy** (1840–1928) wrote about rural life in his novels, poems and short stories. He lived at a time of rapid change in the countryside. Work patterns and social life and attitudes were altering, and he hoped that in his writing he could 'preserve for my own satisfaction a fairly true record of a vanishing life'.

In this story, based on west country folklore, Hardy records the superstitions connected with Midsummer's Eve. Time and place are highly significant. Strange and symbolic events occur, but set within a context of ordinary people living their everyday lives.

'William, as you may know, was a curious, silent man; you could feel when he came near 'ee; and if he was in the house or anywhere behind your back without your seeing him, there seemed to be something clammy in the air, as if a cellar door was opened close by your elbow. Well, one Sunday, at a time that William was in very good health to all appearance, the bell that was ringing for church went very heavy all of a sudden; the sexton, who told me o't, said he'd not known the bell go so heavy in his hand for years – and he feared it meant a death in the parish. That was on the Sunday, as I say. During the week after, it chanced that William's wife was staying up late one night to finish her ironing, she doing the washing for Mr and Mrs Hardcome. Her husband had finished his supper and gone to bed as usual some hour or two before. While she ironed she heard him coming downstairs; he stopped to put on his boots at the stair-foot, where he always left them, and then came on into the living-room where she was ironing, passing through it towards the door, this being the only way from the staircase to the outside of the house. No word was said on either side, William not being a man given to much speaking, and his wife being occupied with her work. He went out and closed the door behind him. As her husband had now and then gone out in this way at night before when unwell, or unable to sleep for want of a pipe, she took no particular notice, and continued at her ironing. This she finished shortly after, and as he had not come in she waited a while for him, putting away the irons and things, and preparing the table for his breakfast in the morning. Still he did not return, and supposing him not far off, and wanting to get to bed herself, tired as she was, she left the door unbarred and went to the stairs, after writing on the back of the door with chalk: *Mind and do the door* (because he was a forgetful man).

'To her great surprise, and I might say alarm, on reaching the foot of the stairs his boots were standing there as they always stood when he had gone to rest; going up to their chamber she found him in bed sleeping as sound as a rock. How he could have got back again without her seeing him was beyond her comprehension. It could only have been by passing behind her very quietly while she was bumping with the iron. But this notion did not satisfy her: it was surely impossible that she should not have seen him come in through a room so small. She could not unravel the mystery, and felt very queer and uncomfortable about it. However, she would not disturb him to question him then, and went to bed herself.

'He rose and left for his work very early the next morning, before she was awake, and she waited his return to breakfast with much anxiety for an explanation, for thinking over the matter by daylight made it seem only the more startling. When he came in to the meal he said, before she could put her question, "What's the meaning of them words chalked on the door?"

'She told him, and asked him about his going out the night before. William declared that he had never left the bedroom after entering it, having in fact undressed, lain down, and fallen asleep directly, never once waking till the clock struck five, and he rose up to go to his labour.

'Betty Privett was as certain in her own mind that he did go out as she was of her own existence, and was little less certain that he did not return. She felt too disturbed to argue with him, and let the subject drop as though she must have been mistaken. When she was walking down Longpuddle street later in the day she met Jim Weedle's daughter Nancy, and said, "Well, Nancy, you do look sleepy today!"

'"Yes, Mrs Privett," says Nancy. "Now don't tell anybody, but I don't mind letting you know what the reason o't is. Last night, being Old Midsummer Eve, some of us went to church porch, and didn't get home till near one."

'"Did ye?" says Mrs Privett. "Old Midsummer yesterday, was it? Faith I didn't think whe'r 'twas Midsummer or Michaelmas; I'd too much work to do.'

'"Yes. And we were frightened enough, I can tell 'ee, by what we saw."

'"What did ye see?"

'(You may not remember, sir, having gone off to foreign parts so young, that on Midsummer Night it is believed hereabout that the faint shapes of all the folk in the parish who are going to be at death's door within the year can be seen entering the church. Those who get over their illness come out again after a while; those that are doomed to die do not return.)

'"What did you see?" asked William's wife.

'"Well," says Nancy, backwardly – "we needn't tell what we saw, or who we saw."

'"You saw my husband," says Betty Privett, in a quiet way.

'"Well, since you put it so," says Nancy, hanging fire, "we – thought we did see him; but it was darkish, and we was frightened, and of course it might not have been he."

'"Nancy, you needn't mind letting it out, though 'tis kept back in kindness. And he didn't come out of the church again: I know it as well as you."

'Nancy did not answer yes or no to that, and no more was said. But three days after, William Privett was mowing with John Chiles in Mr Hardcome's meadow, and in the heat of the day they sat down to eat their bit o' nunch under a tree, and empty their flagon. Afterwards both of 'em fell asleep as they sat. John Chiles was the first to wake, and as he looked towards his fellow-mower he saw one of those great white miller's-souls as we call 'em – that is to say, a miller-moth – come from William's open mouth while he slept, and fly straight away. John thought it odd enough, as William had worked in a mill for several years when he was a boy. He then looked at the sun, and found by the place o't that they had slept a long while, and as William did not wake, John called him and said it was high time to begin work again. He took no notice, and then John went up and shook him, and found he was dead.

'Now on that very day old Philip Hookhorn was down at Longpuddle Spring dipping up a pitcher of water; and as he turned away, who should he see but William, looking very pale and odd. This surprised Philip Hookhorn very much, for years before that time William's little son – his only child – had been drowned in that spring while at play there, and this had so preyed upon William's mind that he'd never been seen near the spring afterwards, and had been known to go half a mile out of his way to avoid the place. On inquiry it was found that William in body could not have stood by the spring, being in the mead two miles off; and it also came out that the time at which he was seen at the spring was the very time when he died.'

# The Violet Car

## E. Nesbit

In several ways, *The Violet Car* is typical of well-told ghost stories. The narrator is a sensible, plain-speaking woman, a nurse who soon gives up the attempt to write in a fancy style. The central characters are consumed by grief; the whole story turns upon what is reality and what is grief-induced imagination. The location and setting of the story are very clearly drawn, and the ending raises as many questions as it settles.

**Edith Nesbit** is best known for her children's books, particularly *The Railway Children* and *The Wouldbegoods*. In fact, she also wrote a great many short stories and articles for adults since her family depended upon her making money from her writing. Edith Nesbit lived from 1858–1924. She was a devoted mother, a keen socialist and party-goer, and a friend of H.G. Wells.

Do you know the downs – the wide windy spaces, the rounded shoulders of the hills leaned against the sky, the hollows where farms and homesteads nestle sheltered, with trees round them pressed close and tight as a carnation in a button-hole? On long summer days it is good to lie on the downs, between short turf and pale, clear sky, to smell the wild thyme, and hear the tiny tinkle of the sheep-bells and the song of the skylark. But on winter evenings when the wind is waking up to its work, spitting rain in your eyes, beating the poor, naked trees and shaking the dusk across the hills like a grey pall, then it is better to be by a warm fireside, in one of the farms that lie lonely where shelter is, and oppose their windows glowing with candle light and firelight to the deepening darkness, as faith holds up its love-lamp in the night of sin and sorrow that is life.

I am unaccustomed to literary effort – and I feel that I shall not say what I have to say, or that it will convince you, unless I say it very plainly. I thought I could adorn my story with pleasant words, prettily arranged. But as I pause to think of what really happened, I see that the plainest words will be the best. I do not know how to weave a plot, nor how to embroider it. It is best not to try. These things happened. I have no skill to add to what happened; nor is any adding of mine needed.

I am a nurse – and I was sent for to go to Charlestown – a mental case. It was November – and the fog was thick in London, so that my cab went at a foot's pace, so I missed the train by which I should have gone. I sent a telegram to Charlestown, and waited in the dismal waiting room at London Bridge. The time was passed for me by a little child. Its mother, a widow, seemed too crushed to be able to respond to its quick questionings. She answered briefly, and not, as it seemed, to the child's satisfaction. The child itself presently seemed to perceive that its mother was not, so to speak, available. It leaned back on the wide, dusty seat and yawned. I caught its eye, and smiled. It would not smile, but it looked. I took out of my bag a silk purse, bright with beads and steel tassels, and turned it over and over. Presently, the child slid along the seat and said, 'Let me' – After that all was easy. The mother sat with eyes closed. When I rose to go, she opened them and thanked me. The child, clinging, kissed me. Later, I saw them get into a first-class carriage in my train. My ticket was a third-class one.

I expected, of course, that there would be a conveyance of some sort to meet me at the station – but there was nothing. Nor was there a cab or a fly to be seen. It was by this time nearly dark, and the wind was driving the rain almost horizontally along the unfrequented road that lay beyond the door of the station. I looked out, forlorn and perplexed.

'Haven't you engaged a carriage?' It was the widow lady who spoke.

I explained.

'My motor will be here directly,' she said, 'you'll let me drive you? Where is it you are going?'

'Charlestown,' I said, and as I said it, I was aware of a very odd change in her face. A faint change, but quite unmistakable.

'Why do you look like that?' I asked her bluntly. And, of course, she said, 'Like what?'

'There's nothing wrong with the house?' I said, for that, I found, was what I had taken that faint change to signify; and I was very young, and one has heard tales. 'No reason why I shouldn't go there, I mean?'

'No – oh no – ' she glanced out through the rain, and I knew as well as though she had told me that there was a reason why *she* should not wish to go there.

'Don't trouble,' I said, 'it's very kind of you – but it's probably out of your way and …'

'Oh – but I'll take you – of *course* I'll take you,' she said, and the child said 'Mother, here comes the car.'

And come it did, though neither of us heard it till the child had spoken. I know nothing of motor cars, and I don't know the names of any of the parts of them. This was like a brougham* – only you got in at the back, as you do in a waggonette; the seats were in the corners, and when the door was shut there was a little seat that pulled up, and the child sat on it between us. And it moved like magic – or like a dream of a train.

We drove quickly through the dark – I could hear the wind screaming, and the wild dashing of the rain against the windows, even through the whirring of the machinery. One could see nothing of the country – only the black night, and the shafts of light from the lamps in front.

After, as it seemed, a very long time, the chauffeur got down and opened a gate. We went through it, and after that the road was very much rougher. We were quite silent in the car, and the child had fallen asleep.

We stopped, and the car stood pulsating as though it were out of breath, while the chauffeur hauled down my box. It was so dark that I could not see the shape of the house, only the lights in the downstairs windows, and the low-walled front garden faintly revealed by their light and the light of the motor lamps. Yet I felt that it was a fair-sized house, that it was

*brougham: type of horse-drawn carriage

surrounded by big trees, and that there was a pond or river close by. In daylight next day I found that all this was so. I have never been able to tell how I knew it that first night, in the dark, but I did know it. Perhaps there was something in the way the rain fell on the trees and on the water. I don't know.

The chauffeur took my box up a stone path, whereon I got out, and said my good-byes and thanks.

'Don't wait, please, don't,' I said. 'I'm all right now. Thank you a thousand times!'

The car, however, stood pulsating till I had reached the doorstep, then it caught its breath, as it were, throbbed more loudly, turned, and went.

And still the door had not opened. I felt for the knocker, and rapped smartly. Inside the door I was sure I heard whispering. The car light was fast diminishing to a little distant star, and its panting sounded now hardly at all. When it ceased to sound at all, the place was quiet as death. The lights glowed redly from curtained windows, but there was no other sign of life. I wished I had not been in such a hurry to part from my escort, from human companionship, and from the great, solid, competent presence of the motor car.

I knocked again, and this time I followed the knock by a shout.

'Hello!' I cried. 'Let me in. I'm the nurse!'

There was a pause, such a pause as would allow time for whisperers to exchange glances on the other side of a door.

Then a bolt ground back, a key turned, and the doorway framed no longer cold, wet wood, but light and a welcoming warmth – and faces.

'Come in, oh, come in,' said a voice, a woman's voice, and the voice of a man said: 'We didn't know there was anyone there.'

And I had shaken the very door with my knockings!

I went in, blinking at the light, and the man called a servant, and between them they carried my box upstairs.

The woman took my arm and led me into a low, square room, pleasant, homely, and comfortable, with solid mid-Victorian comfort – the kind that expressed itself in rep and mahogany. In the lamplight I turned to look at her. She was small and thin, her hair, her face, and her hands were of the same tint of greyish yellow.

'Mrs Eldridge?' I asked.

'Yes,' said she, very softly. 'Oh! I am so glad you've come. I hope you won't be dull here. I hope you'll stay. I hope I shall be able to make you comfortable.'

She had a gentle, urgent way of speaking that was very winning.

'I'm sure I shall be very comfortable,' I said; 'but it's I that am to take care of you. Have you been ill long?'

'It's not me that's ill, really,' she said, 'it's him –'

Now, it was Mr Robert Eldridge who had written to engage me to attend on his wife, who was, he said, slightly deranged.

'I see,' said I. One must never contradict them, it only aggravates their disorder.

'The reason …' she was beginning, when his foot sounded on the stairs, and she fluttered off to get candles and hot water.

He came in and shut the door. A fair, bearded, elderly man, quite ordinary.

'You'll take care of her,' he said. 'I don't want her to get talking to people. She fancies things.'

'What form do the illusions take?' I asked, prosaically.

'She thinks I'm mad,' he said, with a short laugh.

'It's a very usual form. Is that all?'

'It's about enough. And she can't hear things that I can hear, see things that I can see, and she can't smell things. By the way, you didn't see or hear anything of a motor car as you came up, did you?'

'I came up *in* a motor car,' I said shortly. 'You never sent to meet me, and a lady gave me a lift.' I was going to explain about my missing the earlier train, when I found that he was not listening to me. He was watching the door. When his wife came in, with a steaming jug in one hand and a flat candlestick in the other, he went towards her, and whispered eagerly. The only words I caught were: 'She came in a real motor.'

Apparently, to these simple people a motor was as great a novelty as to me. My telegram, by the way, was delivered next morning.

They were very kind to me; they treated me as an honoured guest. When the rain stopped, as it did late the next day, and

I was able to go out, I found that Charlestown was a farm, a large farm, but even to my inexperienced eyes, it seemed neglected and unprosperous. There was absolutely nothing for me to do but to follow Mrs Eldridge, helping her where I could in her household duties, and to sit with her while she sewed in the homely parlour. When I had been in the house a few days, I began to put together the little things that I had noticed singly, and the life at the farm seemed suddenly to come into focus, as strange surroundings do after a while.

I found that I had noticed that Mr and Mrs Eldridge were very fond of each other, and that it was a fondness, and their way of shewing it was a way that told that they had known sorrow, and had borne it together. That she shewed no sign of mental derangement, save in the persistent belief of hers that *he* was deranged. That the morning found them fairly cheerful; that after the early dinner they seemed to grow more and more depressed; that after the 'early cup of tea' – that is just as dusk was falling – they always went for a walk together. That they never asked me to join them in this walk, and that it always took the same direction – across the downs towards the sea. That they always returned from this walk pale and dejected; that she sometimes cried afterwards alone in their bedroom, while he was shut up in the little room they called the office, where he did his accounts, and paid his men's wages, and where his hunting-crops and guns were kept. After supper, which was early, they always made an effort to be cheerful. I knew that this effort was for my sake, and I knew that each of them thought it was good for the other to make it.

Just as I had known before they shewed it to me that Charlestown was surrounded by big trees and had a great pond beside it, so I knew, and in as inexplicable a way, that with these two fear lived. It looked at me out of their eyes. And I knew, too, that this fear was not her fear. I had not been two days in the place before I found that I was beginning to be fond of them both. They were so kind, so gentle, so ordinary, so homely – the kind of people who ought not to have known the name of fear – the kind of people to whom all honest, simple joys should have come by right, and no sorrows but such as come to us all, the death of old friends, and the slow changes of advancing years.

They seemed to belong to the land – to the downs, and the copses, and the old pastures, and the lessening cornfields. I found myself wishing that I, too, belonged to these, that I had been born a farmer's daughter. All the stress and struggle of cram and exam, of school, and college and hospital, seemed so loud and futile, compared with these open secrets of the down life. And I felt this the more, as more and more I felt that I must leave it all – that there was, honestly, no work for me here such as for good or ill I had been trained to do.

'I ought not to stay,' I said to her one afternoon, as we stood at the open door. It was February now, and the snowdrops were thick in tufts beside the flagged path. 'You are quite well.'

'*I* am,' she said.

'You are quite well, both of you,' I said. 'I oughtn't to be taking your money and doing nothing for it.'

'You're doing everything,' she said; 'you don't know how much you're doing.'

'We had a daughter of our own once,' she added vaguely, and then, after a very long pause, she said very quietly and distinctly:

'He has never been the same since.'

'How not the same?' I asked, turning my face up to the thin February sunshine.

She tapped her wrinkled, yellow-grey forehead, as country people do.

'Not right here,' she said.

'How?' I asked. 'Dear Mrs Eldridge, tell me; perhaps I could help somehow.'

Her voice was so sane, so sweet. It had come to this with me, that I did not know which of those two was the one who needed my help.

'He sees things that no one else sees, and hear things no one else hears, and smells things that you can't smell if you're standing there beside him.'

I remembered with a sudden smile his words to me on the morning of my arrival:

'She can't see, or hear, or smell.'

And once more I wondered to which of the two I owed my service.

'Have you any idea why?' I asked. She caught at my arm.

'It was after our Bessie died,' she said – 'the very day she was buried. The motor that killed her – they said it was an accident – it was on the Brighton Road. It was a violet colour. They go into mourning for Queens with violet, don't they?' she added; 'and my Bessie, she was a Queen. So the motor was violet: That was all right, wasn't it?'

I told myself now that I saw that the woman was not normal, and I saw why. It was grief that had turned her brain. There must have been some change in my look, though I ought to have known better, for she said suddenly, 'No. I'll not tell you any more.'

And then he came out. He never left me alone with her for very long. Nor did she ever leave him for very long alone with me.

I did not intend to spy upon them, though I am not sure that my position as nurse to one mentally afflicted would not have justified such spying. But I did not spy. It was chance. I had been to the village to get some blue sewing silk for a blouse I was making, and there was a royal sunset which tempted me to prolong my walk. That was how I found myself on the high downs where they slope to the broken edge of England – the sheer, white cliffs against which the English Channel beats for ever. The furze was in flower, and the skylarks were singing, and my thoughts were with my own life, my own hopes and dreams. So I found that I had struck a road, without knowing when I had struck it. I followed it towards the sea, and quite soon it ceased to be a road, and merged in the pathless turf as a stream sometimes disappears in sand. There was nothing but turf and furze bushes, the song of the skylarks, and beyond the slope that ended at the cliff's edge, the booming of the sea. I turned back, following the road, which defined itself again a few yards back, and presently sank to a lane, deep-banked and bordered with brown hedge stuff. It was there that I came upon them in the dusk. And I heard their voices before I saw them, and before it was possible for them to see me. It was her voice that I heard first.

'No, no, no, no, no,' it said.

'I tell you yes,' that was his voice; 'there – can't you hear it, that panting sound – right away – away? It must be at the very edge of the cliff.'

'There's nothing dearie,' she said, 'indeed there's nothing.'

'You're deaf – and blind – stand back I tell you, it's close upon us.'

I came round the corner of the lane then, and as I came, I saw him catch her arm and throw her against the hedge – violently, as though the danger he feared were indeed close upon them. I stopped behind the turn of the hedge and stepped back. They had not seen me. Her eyes were on his face, and they held a world of pity, love, agony – his face was set in a mask of terror, and his eyes moved quickly as though they followed down the lane the swift passage of something – something that neither she nor I could see. Next moment he was cowering, pressing his body into the hedge – his face hidden in his hands, and his whole body trembling so that I could see it, even from where I was a dozen yards away, through the light screen of the overgrown hedge.

'And the smell of it' he said, 'do you mean to tell me you can't smell it?'

She had her arms round him.

'Come home, dearie,' she said. 'Come home! It's all your fancy – come home with your old wife that loves you.'

They went home.

Next day I asked her to come to my room to look at the new blue blouse. When I had shown it to her I told her, what I had seen and heard yesterday in the lane.

'And now I know,' I said, 'which of you it is that wants care.'

To my amazement she said very eagerly, 'Which?'

'Why, he – of course' – I told her, 'there was nothing there.'

She sat down in the chintz covered armchair by the window, and broke into wild weeping. I stood by her and soothed her as well as I could.

'It's a comfort to know,' she said at last, 'I haven't known what to believe. Many a time, lately, I've wondered whether after all it could be me that was mad, like he said. And there was nothing there? There always *was* nothing there – and it's on him the judgement, not on me. On him. Well, that's something to be thankful for.'

So her tears, I told myself, had been more of relief at her own escape. I looked at her with distaste, and forgot that I had been fond of her. So that her next words cut me like little knives.

'It's bad enough for him as it is,' she said, 'but it's nothing to what it would be for him, if I was really to go off my head and him left to think he'd brought it on me. You see, now I can look after him the same as I've always done. It's only once in the day it comes over him. He couldn't bear it, if it was all the time – like it'll be for me now. It's much better it should be him – I'm better able to bear it than he is.'

I kissed her then and put my arms round her, and said, 'Tell me what it is that frightens him so – and it's every day, you say?'

'Yes – ever since … I'll tell you. It's a sort of comfort to speak out. It was a violet-coloured car that killed our Bessie. You know, our girl that I've told you about. And it's a violet-coloured car that he thinks he sees – every day up there in the lane. And he says he hears it, and that he smells the smell of the machinery – the stuff they put in it – you know.'

'Petrol?'

'Yes, and you can *see* he hears it, and you can *see* he sees it. It haunts him, as if it was a ghost. You see, it was he that picked her up after the violet car went over her. It was that that turned him. I only saw her as he carried her in, in his arms – and then he'd covered her face. But he saw her just as they'd left her, lying in the dust … you could see the place on the road where it happened for days and days.'

'Didn't they come back?'

'Oh yes … they came back. But Bessie didn't come back. But there was a judgement on them. The very night of the funeral, that violet car went over the cliff – dashed to pieces – every soul in it. That was the man's widow that drove you home the first night.'

'I wonder she uses a car after that,' I said – I wanted something commonplace to say.

'Oh,' said Mrs Eldridge, 'it's all what you're used to. We don't stop walking because our girl was killed on the road. Motoring comes as natural to them as walking to us. There's my old man calling – poor old dear. He wants me to go out with him.'

She went, all in a hurry, and in her hurry slipped on the stairs and twisted her ankle. It all happened in a minute and it was a bad sprain.

When I had bound it up, and she was on the sofa, she looked at him, standing as if he were undecided, staring out of the window, with his cap in his hand. And she looked at me.

'Mr Eldridge mustn't miss his walk,' she said. 'You go with him, my dear. A breath of air will do you good.'

So I went, understanding as well as though he had told me, that he did not want me with him, and that he was afraid to go alone, and that he yet had to go.

We went up the lane in silence. At that corner he stopped suddenly, caught my arm, and dragged me back. His eyes followed something that I could not see. Then he exhaled a held breath, and said, 'I thought I heard a motor coming.' He had found it hard to control his terror, and I saw beads of sweat on his forehead and temples. Then we went back to the house.

The sprain was a bad one. Mrs Eldridge had to rest, and again next day it was I who went with him to the corner of the lane.

This time he could not, or did not try to, conceal what he felt. 'There – listen!' he said. 'Surely you can hear it?'

I heard nothing.

'Stand back,' he cried shrilly, suddenly, and we stood back close against the hedge.

Again the eyes followed something invisible to me, and again the held breath exhaled.

'It will kill me one of these days,' he said, 'and I don't know that I care how soon – if it wasn't for her.'

'Tell me,' I said, full of that importance, that conscious competence, that one feels in the presence of other people's troubles. He looked at me.

'I will tell you, by God,' he said. 'I couldn't tell *her*. Young lady, I've gone so far as wishing myself a Roman, for the sake of a priest to tell it to. But I can tell *you*, without losing my soul more than it's lost already. Did you ever hear tell of a violet car that got smashed up – went over the cliff?'

'Yes,' I said. 'Yes.'

'The man that killed my girl was new to the place. And he hadn't any eyes – or ears – or he'd have known me, seeing we'd been face to face at the inquest. And you'd have thought he'd have stayed at home that one day, with the blinds drawn down. But not he. He was swirling and swivelling all about the country in his cursed violet car, the very time we were burying her. And at dusk – there was a mist coming up – he comes up behind me in this very lane, and I stood back, and he pulls up, and he calls out, with his damned lights full in my face: '"Can you tell me the way to Hexham, my man?" says he.

'I'd have liked to shew him the way to hell. And that was the way for me, not him. I don't know how I came to do it. I didn't mean to do it. I didn't think I was going to – and before I knew anything, I'd said it. "Straight ahead," I said; "keep straight ahead." Then the motor-thing panted, chuckled, and he was off. I ran after him to try to stop him – but what's the use of running after these motor-devils? And he kept straight on. And every day since then, every dear day, the car comes by, the violet car that nobody can see but me and it keeps straight on.'

'You ought to go away,' I said, speaking as I had been trained to speak. 'You fancy these things. You probably fancied the whole thing. I don't suppose you ever *did* tell the violet car to go straight ahead. I expect it was all imagination, and the shock of your poor daughter's death. You ought to go right away.'

'I can't,' he said earnestly. 'If I did, some one else would see the car. You see, somebody *has* to see it every day as long as I live. If it wasn't me, it would be someone else. And I'm the only person who *deserves* to see it. I wouldn't like any one else to see it – it's too horrible. *It's* much more horrible than you think,' he added slowly.

I asked him, walking beside him down the quiet lane, what it was that was so horrible about the violet car. I think I quite expected him to say that it was splashed with his daughter's blood ... What he did say was, 'It's too horrible to tell you,' and he shuddered.

I was young then, and youth always thinks it can move mountains. I persuaded myself that I could cure him of his delusion by attacking – not the main fort – that is always, to begin with, impregnable, but one, so to speak, of the outworks. I set myself to persuade him not to go to that corner in the lane, at that hour in the afternoon.

'But if I don't, someone else will see it.'

'There'll be nobody there *to* see it,' I said briskly.

'Someone will be there. Mark my words, someone will be there – and then they'll know.'

'Then I'll be the someone,' I said. 'Come – you stay at home with your wife, and *I'll* go – and if I see it I'll promise to tell you, and if I don't – well, then I will be able to go away with a clear conscience.'

'A clear conscience,' he repeated.

I argued with him in every moment when it was possible to catch him alone. I put all my will and all my energy into my persuasions. Suddenly, like a door that you've been trying to open, and that has resisted every key till the last one, he gave way. Yes – I should go to the lane. And he would not go.

I went.

Being, as I said before, a novice in the writing of stories, I perhaps haven't made you understand that it was quite hard for me to go – that I felt myself at once a coward and a heroine. This business of an imaginary motor that only one poor old farmer could see, probably appears to you quite commonplace and ordinary. It was not so with me. You see, the idea of this thing had dominated my life for weeks and months, had dominated it even before I knew the nature of the domination. It was this that was the fear that I had known to walk with these two people, the fear that shared their bed and board, that lay down and rose up with them. The old man's fear of this and his fear of his fear. And the old man was terribly convincing. When one talked with him, it was quite difficult to believe that he was mad, and that there wasn't, and couldn't be, a mysteriously horrible motor that was visible to him, and invisible to other people. And when he said that, if he were not in the lane, someone else would see it – it was easy to say 'Nonsense,' but to think 'Nonsense' was not so easy, and to *feel* 'Nonsense' quite oddly difficult.

I walked up and down the lane in the dusk, wishing not to wonder what might be the hidden horror in the violet car. I would not let blood into my thoughts. I was not going to be fooled by thought transference, or any of those transcendental follies. I was not going to be hypnotized into seeing things.

I walked up the lane – I had promised him to stand near that corner for five minutes, and I stood there in the deepening dusk, looking up towards the downs and the sea. There were pale stars. Everything was very still. Five minutes is a long time. I held my watch in my hand. Four – four and a quarter – four and a half. Five. I turned instantly. And then I saw that *he* had followed me – he was standing a dozen yards away – and his face was turned from me. It was turned towards a motor car that shot up the lane. It came very swiftly, and before it came to where he was, I knew that it was very horrible. I crushed myself back into the crackling bare hedge, as I should have done to leave room for the passage of a real car – though I knew that this one was not real. It looked real – but I knew it was not.

As it neared him, he started back, then suddenly he cried out. I heard him. 'No, no, no, no – no more, no more,' was what he cried, with that he flung himself down on the road in front of the car, and its great tyres passed over him. Then the car shot past me and I saw what the full horror of it was. There was no blood – that was not the horror. The colour of it was, as she had said, violet.

I got to him and got his head up. He was dead. I was quite calm and collected now, and felt that to be so was extremely creditable to me. I went to a cottage where a labourer was having tea – he got some men and a hurdle.

When I told his wife, the first intelligible thing she said was: 'It's better for him. Whatever he did he's paid for now –' So it looks as though she had known – or guessed – more than he thought.

I stayed with her till her death. She did not live long.

You think perhaps that the old man was knocked down and killed by a real motor, which happened to come that way of all ways, at that hour of all hours, and happened to be, of all colours, violet. Well, a real motor leaves its mark on you where it kills you, doesn't it? But when I lifted up that old man's head from the road, there was no mark on him, no blood – no broken bones – his hair was not disordered, nor his dress. I tell you there was not even a speck of mud on him, except where he had touched the road in falling. There were no tyre-marks in the mud.

The motor car that killed him came and went like a shadow. As he threw himself down, it swerved a little so that both its wheels should go over him.

He died, the doctor said, of heart failure. I am the only person to know that he was killed by a violet car, which, having killed him, went noiselessly away towards the sea. And that car was empty – there was no one in it. It was just a violet car that moved along the lanes swiftly and silently, and was empty.

# Harry
## Rosemary Timperley

*Harry* is a chilling story. Its setting is warm and loving, a world of small children and protective parents. Like the other ghost stories in this selection, it is simply told. Conversations are directly reported, and the first person narration gives the reader an insight into the mother's point of view and her increasing anxiety about her child.

Like the other stories, places and times are very significant. Everyday items become highly symbolic. The tension mounts as we move from the everyday world of children playing to the intensity of the supernatural world in which a teenager's life has been cut short by violence.

**Rosemary Timperley**, born in 1920, has been publishing ghost stories since 1952. She has written over one hundred short stories, and is particularly respected for her ghost stories in which the ghosts are usually gentle rather than horrific, but none the less frightening!

Such ordinary things make me afraid. Sunshine. Sharp shadows on grass. White roses. Children with red hair. And the name – Harry. Such an ordinary name.

Yet the first time Christine mentioned the name, I felt a premonition of fear.

She was five years old, due to start school in three months' time. It was a hot, beautiful day and she was playing alone in the garden, as she often did. I saw her lying on her stomach in the grass, picking daisies and making daisy-chains with laborious pleasure. The sun burned on her pale red hair and made her skin look very white. Her big blue eyes were wide with concentration.

Suddenly she looked towards the bush of white roses, which cast its shadow over the grass, and smiled.

'Yes, I'm Christine,' she said. She rose and walked slowly

towards the bush, her little plump legs defenceless and endearing beneath the too short cotton skirt. She was growing fast.

'With my mummy and daddy,' she said clearly. Then, after a pause, 'Oh, but they are my mummy and daddy.'

She was in the shadow of the bush now. It was as if she'd walked out of the world of light into darkness. Uneasy, without knowing why, I called her:

'Chris, what are you doing?'

''Nothing.'

'Come indoors now.'

She said: 'I must go in now. Good-bye,' then walked towards the house.

'Chris, who were you talking to?'

'Harry,' she said.

'Who's Harry?'

'Harry.'

I couldn't get anything else out of her, so I just gave her some cake and milk and read to her until bedtime. As she listened, she stared out at the garden. Once she smiled and waved. It was a relief finally to tuck her up in bed and feel she was safe.

When Jim, my husband, came home I told him about the mysterious 'Harry'. He laughed.

'Oh, she's started that lark, has she?'

'What do you mean, Jim?'

'It's not so very rare for only children to have an imaginary companion. Some kids talk to their dolls. Chris has never been keen on her dolls. She hasn't any brothers or sisters. She hasn't any friends her own age. So she imagines someone.'

'But why has she picked that particular name?'

He shrugged. 'You know how kids pick things up. I don't know what you're worrying about, honestly I don't.'

'Nor do I really. It's just that I feel extra responsible for her. More so than if I were her real mother.'

'I know, but she's all right. Chris is fine. She's a pretty, healthy, intelligent little girl. A credit to you.'

'And to you.'

'In fact, we're thoroughly nice parents!'

'And so modest!'

We laughed together and he kissed me. I felt consoled.

Until next morning.

Again the sun shone brilliantly on the small, bright lawn and white roses. Christine was sitting on the grass, cross-legged, staring towards the rose bush, smiling.

'Hello,' she said. 'I hoped you'd come ... Because I like you. How old are you? ... I'm only five and a piece ... I'm not a baby! I'm going to school soon and I shall have a new dress. A green one. Do you go to school? ... What do you do then?' She was silent for a while, nodding, listening, absorbed.

I felt myself going cold as I stood there in the kitchen. 'Don't be silly. Lots of children have an imaginary companion,' I told myself desperately. 'Just carry on as if nothing were happening. Don't be a fool.'

But I called Chris in earlier than usual for her mid-morning milk.

'Can Harry come too?'

'No!' The cry burst from me harshly.

'Goodbye, Harry. I'm sorry you can't come in but I've got to have my milk,' Chris said, then ran towards the house.

'Why can't Harry have some milk too?' she challenged me.

'Who *is* Harry, darling?'

'Harry's my brother.'

'But Chris, you haven't got a brother. Daddy and Mummy have only got one child, one little girl, that's you. Harry can't be your brother.'

'Harry's my brother. He says so.' She bent over the glass of milk and emerged with a smeary top lip. Then she grabbed at the plate of biscuits. At least 'Harry' hadn't spoilt her appetite!

I didn't mention any of this to Jim that night. I know he'd only scoff as he'd done before. But when Christine's 'Harry' fantasy went on day after day, I found it got more and more on my nerves.

One Sunday, when Jim heard her at it he said:

'I'll say one thing for imaginary companions, they help a child on with her talking. Chris is talking much more freely than she used to.'

'With an accent,' I blurted out.

'An accent?'

'A slight cockney accent.'

'My dearest, every London child gets a slight cockney accent. It'll be much worse when she goes to school and meets lots of other kids.'

'We don't talk cockney. Where does she get it from? Who can she be getting it from except Ha – ?' I couldn't say the name.

'The baker, the milkman, the dustman, the coalman, the window cleaner – want any more?'

'I suppose not.' I laughed rather ruefully.

'Do you know what I think you should do to put your mind at rest?'

'What?'

'Take Chris along to see old Dr Webster tomorrow. Let him have a little talk with her.'

'Do you think she's ill – in her mind?'

'Good heavens, no! But when we come across something that's beyond us, it's as well to take professional advice.'

Next day I took Christine to see Dr Webster. I left her in the waiting-room while I told him briefly about Harry. He nodded sympathetically, then he said:

'It's a fairly unusual case, Mrs James, but by no means unique. I've had several cases of children's imaginary companions becoming so real to them that the parents got the jitters. Christine is rather a lonely little girl, isn't she?'

'She doesn't know any other children. We're new to the neighbourhood, you see. But that will be put right when she starts school.'

'And I think you'll find that when she goes to school and meets other children, these fantasies will disappear. You see, every child needs company of her own age, and if she doesn't get it, she invents it. Older people who are lonely talk to themselves. That doesn't mean that they're crazy, just that they need to talk to someone. A child is more practical. Seems silly to talk to oneself, she thinks, so she invents someone to talk to. I honestly don't think you've anything to worry about.'

'That's what my husband says.'

'I'm sure he does. Still, I'll have a chat with Christine as you've brought her. Leave us alone together.'

I went to the waiting-room to fetch Chris. She was at the window. She said: 'Harry's waiting.'

'Where, Chris?' I said quietly.

'There. By the rose bush.'

The doctor had a bush of white roses in his garden.

'There's no one there,' I said. Chris gave me a glance of un-childlike scorn. 'Dr Webster wants to see you now, darling,' I said shakily. 'You remember him, don't you? He gave you sweets when you were getting better from chicken pox.'

'Yes,' she said and went willingly enough to the doctor's surgery. I waited restlessly. Faintly I heard their voices through the wall, heard the doctor's chuckle, Christine's high peal of laughter. She was talking away to the doctor in a way she didn't talk to me.

When they came out, he said: 'Nothing wrong with her whatever. She's just an imaginative little monkey. A word of advice, Mrs James. Let her talk about Harry. Let her become accustomed to confiding in you. I gather you've shown some disapproval of this "brother" of hers so she doesn't talk much to you about him. He makes wooden toys, doesn't he, Chris?'

'Yes, Harry makes wooden toys.'

'And he can read and write, can't he?'

'And swim and climb trees and paint pictures. Harry can do everything. He's a wonderful brother.' Her little face flushed with adoration.

The doctor patted me on the shoulder and said: 'Harry sounds a very nice brother for her. He's even got red hair like you, Chris, hasn't he?'

'Harry's got red hair,' said Chris proudly, 'redder than my hair. And he's nearly as tall as daddy, only thinner. He's as tall as you, mummy. He's fourteen. He says he's tall for his age. What is tall for his age?'

'Mummy will tell you about that as you walk home,' said Dr Webster. 'Now, goodbye, Mrs James. Don't worry. Just let her prattle. Goodbye, Chris. Give my love to Harry.'

Another week passed. It was Harry, Harry all the time. The

day before she was to start school, Chris said: 'Not going to school.'

'You're going to school tomorrow, Chris. You're looking forward to it. You know you are. There'll be lots of other little girls and boys.'

'Harry says he can't come too.'

'You won't want Harry at school. He'll –' I tried hard to follow the doctor's advice and appear to believe in Harry – 'He'll be too old. He'd feel silly among little boys and girls, a great lad of fourteen.'

'I won't go to school without Harry. I want to be with Harry.' She began to weep, loudly, painfully.

She slept with tearstains still on her face.

It was still daylight. I went to the window to draw the curtains. Golden shadows and long strips of sunshine in the garden. Then, almost like a dream, the long thin clear-cut shadow of a boy near the white roses. Like a mad woman I opened the window and shouted: 'Harry! Harry!'

I thought I saw a glimmer of red among the roses, like close red curls on a boy's head. Then there was nothing.

Next day I started on my secret mission. I took a bus to town and went to the big, gaunt building I hadn't visited for over five years. Then, Jim and I had gone together. The top floor of the building belonged to the Greythorne Adoption Society. I climbed the four flights and knocked on the familiar door with its scratched paint.

Miss Cleaver, a tall, thin grey-haired woman with a charming smile, a plain, kindly face and a very wrinkled brow, rose to meet me. 'Mrs James. How nice to see you again. How's Christine?'

'She's very well. Miss Cleaver, I'd better get straight to the point. I know you don't normally divulge the origin of a child to its adopters and vice versa, but I must know who Christine is.'

'Sorry, Mrs James,' she began, 'our rules ...'

'Please let me tell you the whole story, then you'll see I'm not just suffering from vulgar curiosity.'

I told her about Harry.

When I'd finished she said: 'It's very queer. Very queer

indeed. Mrs James, I'm going to break my rule for once. I'm going to tell you in confidence where Christine came from.

'She was born in a very poor part of London. There were four in the family, father, mother, son, and Christine herself.'

'Son?'

'Yes. He was fourteen when – when it happened.'

'When what happened?'

'Let me start at the beginning. The parents hadn't really wanted Christine. The family lived in one room at the top of an old house which should have been condemned by the Sanitary Inspector in my opinion. It was difficult enough when there were only three of them, but with a baby as well life became a nightmare. The mother was a neurotic creature, slatternly, unhappy, too fat. After she'd had the baby she took no interest in it. The brother, however, adored the little girl from the start. He got into trouble for cutting school so he could look after her.

'One morning in the small hours, a woman in the ground-floor room saw something fall past her window and heard a thud on the ground. She went out to look. The son of the family was there on the ground. Christine was in his arms. The boy's neck was broken. He was dead. Christine was blue in the face but still breathing faintly.

'The woman woke the household, sent for the police and the doctor, then they went to the top room. They had to break down the door, which was locked and sealed inside. An overpowering smell of gas greeted them, in spite of the open window.

'They found husband and wife dead in bed and a note from the husband saying:

"*I can't go on. I am going to kill them all. It's the only way*."

'The police concluded that he'd sealed up door and windows and turned on the gas when his family were asleep, then lain beside his wife until he drifted into unconsciousness, and death. But the son must have wakened. Perhaps he struggled with the door but couldn't open it. He'd been too weak to shout. All he could do was pluck away the seals from the window, open it, and fling himself out, holding his adored little sister tightly in his arms.'

'So her brother saved her life and died himself?' I said.

'Yes. He was a very brave boy.'

'Perhaps he thought not so much of saving her as of keeping her with him. Oh dear! That sounds ungenerous. I didn't mean to be. Miss Cleaver, what was his name?'

'I'll have to look that up for you.' She referred to one of her many files and said at last: 'The family's name was Jones and the fourteen-year-old brother was called "Harold".'

'And did he have red hair?' I murmured.

'That I don't know, Mrs James.'

'But it's Harry. The boy was Harry. What does it mean? I can't understand it.'

'It's not easy, but I think perhaps deep in her unconscious mind Christine has always remembered Harry, the companion of her babyhood. We don't think of children as having much memory, but there must be images of the past tucked away somewhere in the little heads. Christine doesn't invent this Harry. She *remembers* him. So clearly that she's almost brought him to life again.'

'May I have the address of the house where they lived?'

The house seemed deserted. It was filthy and derelict. But one thing made me stare and stare. There was a tiny garden. A scatter of bright uneven grass splashed the bald brown patches of earth. But the little garden had one strange glory that none of the other houses in the poor sad street possessed – a bush of white roses.

A voice startled me: 'What are you doing here?' It was an old woman, peering from the ground-floor window.

'I thought the house was empty,' I said.

'Should be. Been condemned. But they can't get me out. Nowhere else to go. Won't go. The others went quickly enough after it happened. No one else wants to come. They say the place is haunted. So it is. But what's the fuss about? Life and death. They're very close. You get to know that when you're old. Alive or dead. What's the difference?'

She looked at me with yellowish, bloodshot eyes and said: 'I saw him fall past my window. That's where he fell. Among the roses. He still comes back. I see him. He won't go away until he gets her.'

'Who – who are you talking about?'

'Harry Jones. Nice boy he was. Red hair. Very thin. Too determined though. Always got his own way. Loved Christine too much, I thought. Died among the roses. Used to sit down here with her for hours, by the roses. Then he died there. Or do people die? The church ought to give us an answer, but it doesn't. Not one you can believe. Go away, will you? This place isn't for you. It's for the dead who aren't dead, and the living who aren't alive.'

The crazy eyes staring at me beneath the matted white fringe of hair frightened me. Mad people are terrifying. One can pity them, but one is still afraid. I murmured:

'I'll go now. Goodbye,' and tried to hurry across the hard hot pavements although my legs felt heavy and half-paralysed, as in a nightmare.

The sun blazed down on my head, but I was hardly aware of it. I lost all sense of time or place as I stumbled on.

Then I heard something that chilled my blood.

A clock struck three.

At three o'clock I was supposed to be at the school gates, waiting for Christine.

Where was I now? How near the school? What bus should I take?

I made frantic inquiries of passers-by, who looked at me fearfully, as I had looked at the old woman.

At last I caught the right bus and, sick with dust, petrol fumes and fear, reached the school. I ran across the hot, empty playground. In a classroom, the young teacher in white was gathering her books together.

'I've come for Christine James. I'm her mother. I'm so sorry I'm late. Where is she?' I gasped.

'Christine James?' The girl frowned, then said brightly: 'Oh yes, I remember, the pretty little red-haired girl. That's all right, Mrs James. Her brother called for her. How alike they are, aren't they? And so devoted. It's rather sweet to see a boy of that age so fond of his baby sister. Has your husband got red hair, like the two children?'

'What did – her brother – say?' I asked faintly.

'He didn't say anything. When I spoke to him, he just smiled. They'll be home by now, I should think. I say, do you feel all right?'

'Yes, thank you. I must go home.'

I ran all the way home through the burning streets.

'Chris! Christine, where are you? Chris! Chris!' Sometimes even now I hear my own voice of the past screaming through the cold house. 'Christine! Chris! Where are you? Answer me! Chrrriiiiss!' Then: 'Harry! Don't take her away! Come back! Harry! Harry!'

Demented, I rushed out into the garden. The sun struck me like a hot blade. The roses glared whitely. The air was so still I seemed to stand in timelessness, placelessness. For a moment, I seemed very near to Christine, although I couldn't see her. Then the roses danced before my eyes and turned red. The world turned red. Blood red. Wet red. I fell through the redness to blackness to nothingness.

For weeks I was in bed with sunstroke which turned to brain fever. During that time Jim and the police searched for Christine in vain. The futile search continued for months. The papers were full of the strange disappearance of the red-haired child. The teacher described the 'brother' who had called for her. There were newspaper stories of kidnapping, baby-snatching, child-murders. Then the sensation died down. It became just another unsolved mystery in police files.

And only two people knew what had happened. An old crazed woman living in a derelict house, and myself.

Years have passed. But I walk in fear.

Such ordinary things make me afraid. Sunshine. Sharp shadows on grass. White roses. Children with red hair. And the name – Harry. Such an ordinary name!

# Crossing Over
## Catherine Storr

Catherine Storr's fiction often has an interesting psychological angle to it, which is not surprising since she is both a writer and a psychiatrist. The story included in this collection, ambiguously titled *Crossing Over*, gives us an insider's view of how the main character is thinking and feeling.

As with the other stories, the setting is very ordinary. The girl seems quite ordinary and is not even given a name. The incident being described is an everyday event – walking a dog. The story is told in a simple, matter-of-fact way which makes the readers think they understand what is happening. But the response of Mrs Matthews and her dog Togo at the end of the story make us see events rather differently.

If she hadn't been fond of dogs, she would never have volunteered for this particular job. When her class at school were asked if they would give up some of their spare time towards helping old people, most of the tasks on offer had sounded dreary. Visiting housebound old men and women, making them cups of tea and talking to them; she hadn't fancied that, and she wasn't any good at making conversation, let alone being able to shout loud enough for a deaf person to hear. Her voice was naturally quiet. She didn't like the idea of doing anyone else's shopping, she wasn't good enough at checking that she'd got the right change. The check-out girls in the supermarket were too quick, ringing up the different items on the cash register. Nor did she want to push a wheelchair to the park. But walking old Mrs Matthews' dog, that had seemed like something she might even enjoy. She couldn't go every evening, but she would take him for a good long run on the Common on Saturdays, and on fine evenings, when the days were longer, she'd try to call for him after school some weekdays. She had started out full of enthusiasm.

What she hadn't reckoned with was the dog himself. Togo was huge, half Alsatian, half something else which had given him long woolly hair, permanently matted and dirty. Once, right at the beginning, she had offered to bathe and groom him, but Mrs Matthews had been outraged by the suggestion, was sure the poor creature would catch cold, and at the sight of the comb Togo backed and growled and showed his teeth. It was as much as she could do to fasten and unfasten his leash, and he did not make that easy. The early evening walks weren't quite so bad, because there wasn't time to take him to the Common, so he stayed on the leash all the time. Even then he was difficult to manage. He seemed to have had no training and he certainly had no manners. He never stopped when she told him to, never came when she called him, so that every Saturday, when she dutifully let him run free among the gorse bushes and little trees on the Common, she was afraid she might have to return to Mrs Matthews without the dog, confessing that he had run away. Mrs Matthews did not admit that Togo was unruly and difficult to manage, any more than she would admit that he smelled. It was only a feeling that she shouldn't go back on her promise to perform this small service to the community that kept the girl still at the disagreeable task.

This particular evening was horrible. She'd been kept later at school than usual, and although it was already March, the sky was overcast, it was beginning to get dark, and a fine drizzling rain made the pavements slippery. Togo was in a worse mood than usual. He had slouched along, stopping for whole minutes at lampposts and dustbins and misbehaving extravagantly in the most inconvenient places, in spite of her frantic tugs at the leash to try to get him off the pavement. He was too strong for her to control, and he knew it. She almost believed that he had a spite against her, and enjoyed showing that he didn't have to do anything she wanted, as if it wasn't bad enough having to go out in public with an animal so unkempt and anti-social.

They reached the zebra crossing on the hill. The traffic was moving fast, as it always did during the evening rush-hour. She would have to wait for a break before she could step off the pavement, especially as, in the half dark, she knew from her

Dad's comments when he was driving, pedestrians on the road were not easy to see. She stood still and dragged at Togo's lead. But Togo did not mean to be dictated to by a little schoolgirl, and after a moment's hesitation, he pulled too. He was off, into the middle of the oncoming traffic, wrenching at the leash, which she had twisted round her hand in order to get a better grip. She threw all her weight against his, but she was no match for him. She thought she felt the worn leather snap, she heard the sound of screaming brakes and someone shouted. She had time to think, 'What am I going to say to Mrs Matthews?', before her head swam and she thought she was going to faint.

She found herself standing on the further side of the road. She saw a huddle of people, surrounding stationary cars. Two drivers had left their vehicles and were abusing each other. As the crowd swayed, she saw the bonnet of a red car crumpled by its contact with the back of a large yellow van. She saw, too, a dark stain on the road surface. Blood. Blood made her feel sick and her head swam again. She hesitated, knowing that she ought to go among the watching people to make herself look, perhaps to try to explain how Togo had pulled, how she hadn't been strong enough to hold him back. Someone should be told whose dog he was. Someone would have to go and break the terrible news to Mrs Matthews.

As she was considering this, she heard the siren of a police car and the two-note call of an ambulance. She thought, 'Perhaps someone got badly hurt in one of the cars, and it's all my fault.' Her courage evaporated, and she turned away from the accident and began to walk, on legs that trembled, up the hill towards her own home. She thought, 'I'll go and tell Mum.' But then she remembered how much Mrs Matthews loved horrible Togo, how she talked about him as her only friend, and how dreadful it was going to be for her to open her front door to find a policeman telling her that her dog was dead. Besides, the policeman might say that it was all her, the girl's, fault. She had to go first to Mrs Matthew's house, to break the news gently, and also to explain that she had tried her best to prevent the accident.

She found that she must have been walking really fast, which was surprising, considering how much she was dreading the ordeal in front of her. She had reached the grocer's and the newspaper shop at the top of the High Street almost before she'd realized. She saw Sybil Grainger coming out of the newspaper shop, and she was ready to say, 'Hi!' and to pretend that there was nothing wrong, but luckily Sybil seemed not to have seen her. She turned the corner into Grange Road, relieved that she hadn't had to carry on a conversation. Grange Road also seemed shorter than usual; now she had to go along Fenton Crescent till she reached the small side street where Mrs Matthews lived, in one of the row of little old cottages known as Paradise Row.

Her heart beat furiously as she unlatched the small wooden gate and walked the short distance up to the front door, rehearsing exactly how to say what she had to. She lifted the knocker. As it came down on the wood, it made a hollow, echoing sound.

Extraordinary. From the other side of the door, she heard something very much like Togo's deep, menacing growl. She must be in such a state of nerves that she was imagining impossible things. Or perhaps when she felt faint out there in the road, she had fallen and hit her head and been concussed. She felt her scalp, under the straight, silky hair, but she couldn't find any tender spots. She waited. Mrs Matthews was arthritic and always took a long time to answer the door and there was no hurry for the message she was going to receive.

Steps came slowly, dragging a little, along the passage. The door opened, and she braced herself for the shock she was about to administer and the scolding she was certainly going to receive.

But when Mrs Matthews looked out, she behaved in a very peculiar way. Instead of saying immediately, 'Where's Togo?' she asked nothing of her visitor, but bent forward and peered out, looking up and down the short row of cottages, as if she were searching for something or someone who might be coming or going in the street. Her head with its thinning grey hair was so close that the girl stepped back, opening her mouth to begin her explanation. But what she saw in the passage behind the old woman stopped her from uttering a sound.

At the further end of the passage was a dog. Togo. Togo, whole, apparently unharmed, his collar round his neck, and the end of the broken leash still attached, dragging behind him.

For a moment she thought he was going to spring forward and attack her. Then she saw that, instead, he was backing, shrinking as far away as he could get. He was making a curious noise, not a howl, nor a growl, but a sort of whine. She noticed that he was trembling. She had never seen Togo tremble before. He was showing whites round his yellow eyes and the short hair round his muzzle was bristling.

She started to speak. But Mrs Matthews appeared not to have heard her. She was turning to calm the terrified dog. She was saying, 'Whatever's the matter with you, Togo? Think you're seeing a ghost?'

# Ghost: Activities

## 1 Comparing stories for wide reading

Compare and contrast Thomas Hardy's *The Superstitious Man's Story* with
**either**
*The Violet Car* by E. Nesbit
**or**
*Harry* by Rosemary Timperley
**or**
*Crossing Over* by Catherine Storr.

Consider the main similarities and differences in the way the stories are written, and decide which of the stories you find most successful as a ghost story and why.

You might like to comment on:

- The way the stories are told – who the narrator is, the point of view expressed and the style of language used in the telling.
- The use of place in the story.
- The importance of time in the story.
- The relationship between the central characters, and the effect that it has on the supernatural part of the story.
- The underlying emotions that the story is dealing with. Are these portrayed effectively?
- The way the 'ghost' appears and influences events.
- How the ending works. Is it satisfying to readers? Is it ambiguous?
- The use of symbolism in the stories.

## 2 Opportunities for original writing

When you have thought about what you have learned from this section on ghost stories, choose one of the following:

- Write a story from the ghost's point of view. (You might like to keep the reader guessing about whether the narrator is dead or alive until the end.)
- Write a story based on the idea that a character's grief at the death of a loved one is so intense that the dead person seems to return as a ghost.
- Choose a ghostly place and time (such as the church porch at Midsummer Eve in Hardy's story). Describe three separate spooky incidents that take place in the location you have chosen. Give the year and report of the incidents, but remember they could take place hundreds of years apart, and the place will change over the years. Build up the atmosphere of the place and occasion in your description.
- Use diary entries and letters to tell a ghost story.
- Write a comic ghost story about a haunting that goes wrong.
- Write a story about the ghost of a person who lived a thoughtless and selfish life. The ghost is given a last chance to put right some of the damage by being allowed to return to Earth for a limited amount of time. What happens?

Section 2

# Crime and Detection

Stories of crime and detection have been popular for many years. Perhaps this is because of a human fascination with crime. If we see a crowd gathering at the scene of a crime we stop to find out what happened, who was involved and who committed the crime. It is this desire to find out, this basic curiosity to discover 'whodunit', that makes us keep turning the pages when reading detective fiction.

Usually the writer leaves a careful trail of clues for the reader to follow. If we are alert readers we can pick up the clues and solve the puzzle. However, things are not always as they seem and we will often find ourselves distracted by misleading clues – red herrings – which are designed to confuse. This is all part of the fun of reading detective fiction.

Detective fiction also deals with the idea of crime bringing disorder and chaos to an ordered world. Sometimes this is the ordered world of the English village, as in the stories of Agatha Christie and Dorothy Sayers. The middle classes presented there find the comfort and calm of their lives threatened by crime, and look to the detective – often a gifted amateur, sometimes an eccentric brainbox – to restore order to their lives.

At other times the detective might be asked to solve a crime which involves visiting the city, where danger lurks in the shadows. Such stories tend to dramatize the fears of the middle classes concerning crime and violence, always with the reassurance that the crime will be solved and order restored eventually.

Other crime fiction, of the American 'hard-boiled' school, takes as its starting point the grim realities of urban living. In these stories a hard-nosed, professional detective investigates the seamier side of city life, often making no moral judgement about the crime he or she encounters.

# The Man with the Twisted Lip

## Sir Arthur Conan Doyle

Sherlock Holmes is probably the best known fictional detective. He first appeared in a story called *A Study in Scarlet* published in 1887. Narrated by down-to-earth Doctor Watson, the story told how amateur detective Sherlock Holmes used his extraordinary powers of deduction to solve crimes.

This unlikely pairing, of Sherlock Holmes and Dr Watson, was the creation of **Arthur Conan Doyle** (1859–1930), who had originally trained as a doctor at the Edinburgh Royal Infirmary. There he was taught to study his patients through the process of accurate observation and rational deduction. He used this same approach in his writing and so created the 'scientific method' of Sherlock Holmes.

The Sherlock Holmes stories, published in the *Strand* magazine, became enormously popular. The stories were illustrated by Sidney Paget who drew the now familiar 'tall spare figure of Holmes' and gave him the famous deerstalker hat. The huge, rounded meerschaum pipe also became familiar, following a stage production of one of the stories in the 1920s.

Readers of *The Man with the Twisted Lip* will be interested to see the underworld of Victorian London represented so graphically in this story. This is a world of drug addiction, opium dens, 'vile alleys', gin shops, ruffians and beggars. It is a world far away from the comfortable life of Dr Watson who sets out from his 'cheery sitting room' on behalf of a 'young timid woman' to find her husband in an opium den. There, much to Dr Watson's surprise, he also finds Sherlock Holmes, and gets drawn into a story where nothing is quite as it seems. The story is full of unexpected twists and turns and offers a fascinating insight into the anxieties and fears of the period.

Isa Whitney, brother of the late Elias Whitney, D.D., Principal of the Theological College of St George's, was much addicted to opium. The habit grew upon him, as I understand, from some foolish freak when he was at college, for having read De Quincey's description of his dreams and sensations, he had drenched his tobacco with laudanum* in an attempt to produce the same effects. He found, as so many more have done, that the practice is easier to attain than to get rid of, and for many years he continued to be a slave to the drug, an object of mingled horror and pity to his friends and relatives. I can see him now, with yellow, pasty face, drooping lids and pin-point pupils, all huddled in a chair, the wreck and ruin of a noble man.

One night – it was in June, '89 – there came a ring to my bell, about the hour when a man gives his first yawn, and glances at the clock. I sat up in my chair, and my wife laid her needlework down in her lap and made a little face of disappointment.

'A patient!' she said. 'You'll have to go out.'

I groaned, for I was newly come back from a weary day.

We heard the door open, a few hurried words, and then quick steps upon the linoleum. Our own door flew open, and a lady, clad in some dark-coloured stuff, with a black veil, entered the room.

'You will excuse my calling so late,' she began, and then, suddenly losing her self-control, she ran forward, threw her arms about my wife's neck, and sobbed upon her shoulder. 'Oh, I'm in such trouble!' she cried; 'I do so want a little help.'

'Why,' said my wife, pulling up her veil, 'It is Kate Whitney. How you startled me, Kate! I had not an idea who you were when you came in.'

'I didn't know what to do, so I came straight to you.' That was always the way. Folk who were in grief came to my wife like birds to a lighthouse.

'It was very sweet of you to come. Now, you must have some wine and water, and sit here comfortably and tell us all about it. Or should you rather that I sent James off to bed?'

---

*laudanum: opium dissolved in alcohol

'Oh, no, no. I want the Doctor's advice and help too. It's about Isa. He has not been home for two days. I am so frightened about him!'

It was not the first time that she had spoken to us of her husband's trouble, to me as a doctor, to my wife as an old friend and school companion. We soothed and comforted her by such words as we could find. Did she know where her husband was? Was it possible that we could bring him back to her?

It seemed that it was. She had the surest information that of late he had, when the fit was on him, made use of an opium den in the furthest east of the City. Hitherto his orgies had always been confined to one day, and he had come back, twitching and shattered, in the evening. But now the spell had been upon him eight and forty hours, and he lay there, doubtless among the dregs of the docks, breathing in the poison or sleeping off the effects. There he was to be found, she was sure of it, at the 'Bar of Gold,' in Upper Swandam Lane. But what was she to do? How could she, a young and timid woman, make her way into such a place, and pluck her husband out from among the ruffians who surrounded him?

There was the case, and of course there was but one way out of it. Might I not escort her to this place? And, then, as a second thought, why should she come at all? I was Isa Whitney's medical adviser, and as such I had influence over him. I could manage it better if I were alone. I promised her on my word that I would send him home in a cab within two hours if he were indeed at the address which she had given me. And so in ten minutes I had left my armchair and cheery sitting-room behind me, and was speeding eastward in a hansom on a strange errand, as it seemed to me at the time, though the future only could show how strange it was to be.

But there was no great difficulty in the first stage of my adventure. Upper Swandam Lane is a vile alley lurking behind the high wharves which line the north side of the river to the east of London Bridge. Between a slop shop and a gin shop, approached by a steep flight of steps leading down to a black gap like the mouth of a cave, I found the den of which I was in search. Ordering my cab to wait, I passed down the steps, worn hollow in the centre by the ceaseless tread of drunken feet, and by the light of a flickering oil lamp above the door I found the latch and made my way into a long, low room, thick and heavy with the brown opium smoke, and terraced with wooden berths, like the forecastle of an emigrant ship.

Through the gloom one could dimly catch a glimpse of bodies lying in strange fantastic poses, bowed shoulders, bent knees, heads thrown back and chins pointing upwards, with here and there a dark, lack-lustre eye turned upon the newcomer. Out of the black shadows there glimmered little red circles of light, now bright, now faint, as the burning poison waxed or waned in the bowls of the metal pipes. The most lay silent but some muttered to themselves, and others talked together in a strange, low, monotonous voice, their conversation coming in gushes, and then suddenly tailing off into silence, each mumbling out his own thoughts, and paying little heed to the words of his neighbour. At the further end was a small brazier of burning charcoal, beside which on a three-legged stool there sat a tall, thin old man with his jaw resting upon his two fists, and his elbows upon his knees, staring into the fire.

As I entered, a sallow Malay attendant had hurried up with a pipe for me and a supply of the drug, beckoning me to an empty berth.

'Thank you. I have not come to stay,' said I. 'There is a friend of mine here, Mr Isa Whitney, and I wish to speak with him.'

There was a movement and an exclamation from my right, and, peering through the gloom, I saw Whitney, pale, haggard, and unkempt, staring out at me.

'My God! It's Watson,' said he. He was in a pitiable state of reaction, with every nerve in a twitter. 'I say, Watson, what o'clock is it?'

'Nearly eleven.'

'Of what day?'

'Of Friday, June 19th.'

'Good heavens! I thought it was Wednesday. It is Wednesday. What d'you want to frighten a chap for?' He sank his face on to his arms, and began to sob in a high treble key.

'I tell you that it is Friday, man. Your wife has been waiting this two days for you. You should be ashamed of yourself!'

'So I am. But you've got mixed, Watson, for I have only been here a few hours, three pipes, four pipes – I forget how many. But I'll go home with you. I wouldn't frighten Kate – poor little Kate. Give me your hand! Have you a cab?'

'Yes, I have one waiting.'

'Then I shall go in it. But I must owe something. Find what I owe, Watson. I am all off colour. I can do nothing for myself.'

I walked down the narrow passage between the double row of sleepers, holding my breath to keep out the vile, stupefying fumes of the drug, and looking about for the manager. As I passed the tall man who sat by the brazier I felt a sudden pluck at my skirt and a low voice whispered, 'Walk past me, and then look back at me.' The words fell quite distinctly upon my ear. I glanced down. They could only have come from the old man at my side, and yet he sat now as absorbed as ever, very thin, very wrinkled, bent with age, an opium pipe dangling down from between his knees, as though it had dropped in sheer lassitude from his fingers. I took two steps forward and looked back. It took all my self-control to prevent me from breaking out into a cry of astonishment. He had turned his back so that none could see him but I. His form had filled out, his wrinkles were gone, the dull eyes had regained their fire, and there, sitting by the fire, and grinning at my surprise, was none other than Sherlock Holmes. He made a slight motion to me to approach him, and instantly, as he turned his face half round to the company once more, subsided into a doddering, loose-lipped senility.

'Holmes!' I whispered, 'what on earth are you doing in this den?'

'As low as you can,' he answered, 'I have excellent ears. If you would have the great kindness to get rid of that sottish* friend of yours I should be exceedingly glad to have a little talk with you.'

'I have a cab outside.'

'Then pray send him home in it. You may safely trust him, for

---

*sottish: intoxicated by drink or drugs

he appears to be too limp to get into any mischief. I should recommend you also to send a note by the cabman to your wife to say that you have thrown in your lot with me. If you will wait outside, I shall be with you in five minutes.'

It was difficult to refuse any of Sherlock Holmes' requests, for they were always so exceedingly definite, and put forward with such an air of mastery. I felt, however, that when Whitney was once confined in the cab, my mission was practically accomplished; and for the rest, I could not wish anything better than to be associated with my friend in one of those singular adventures which were the normal condition of his existence. In a few minutes I had written my note, paid Whitney's bill, led him out to the cab, and seen him driven through the darkness. In a very short time a decrepit figure had emerged from the opium den, and I was walking down the street with Sherlock Holmes. For two streets he shuffled along with a bent back and an uncertain foot. Then, glancing quickly round, he straightened himself out and burst into a hearty fit of laughter.

'I suppose, Watson,' said he, 'that you imagine that I have added opium-smoking to cocaine injections and all the other little weaknesses on which you have favoured me with your medical views.'

'I was certainly surprised to find you there.'

'But not more so than I to find you.'

'I came to find a friend.'

'And I to find an enemy!'

'An enemy?'

'Yes, one of my natural enemies, or shall I say, my natural prey. Briefly, Watson, I am in the midst of a very remarkable inquiry, and I have hoped to find a clue in the incoherent ramblings of these sots, as I have done before now. Had I been recognized in that den my life would not have been worth an hour's purchase, for I have used it before now for my own purposes, and the rascally Lascar* who runs it has sworn vengeance upon me. There is a trap-door at the back of that building, near the corner of Paul's Wharf, which could

---

Lascar: south-east Asian seaman

tell some strange tales of what has passed through it upon the moonless nights.'

'What! You do not mean bodies?'

'Aye, bodies, Watson. We should be rich men if we had a thousand pounds for every poor devil who has been done to death in that den. It is the vilest murder-trap on the whole river-side, and I fear that Neville St Clair has entered it never to leave it more. But our trap should be here!' He put his two fore-fingers between his teeth and whistled shrilly, a signal which was answered by a similar whistle from the distance, followed shortly by the rattle of wheels and the clink of horse's hoofs. 'Now, Watson,' said Holmes, as a tall dog-cart dashed up through the gloom, throwing out two golden tunnels of yellow light from its side lanterns, 'you'll come with me, won't you?'

'If I can be of use.'

'Oh, a trusty comrade is always of use. And a chronicler still more so. My room at The Cedars is a double-bedded one.'

'The Cedars?'

'Yes; that is Mr St Clair's house. I am staying there while I conduct the inquiry.'

'Where is it, then?'

'Near Lee, in Kent. We have a seven-mile drive before us.'

'But I am all in the dark.'

'Of course you are. You'll know all about it presently. Jump up here! All right, John, we shall not need you. Here's half-a-crown. Look out for me to-morrow, about eleven. Give her her head! So long, then!'

He flicked the horse with his whip, and we dashed away through the endless succession of sombre and deserted streets, which widened gradually, until we were flying across a broad balustraded bridge, with the murky river flowing sluggishly beneath us. Beyond lay another broad wilderness of bricks and mortar, its silence broken only by the heavy, regular footfall of the policeman, or the songs and shouts of some belated party of revellers. A dull wrack* was drifting slowly

---

*wrack: ragged cloud formation

across the sky, and a star or two twinkled dimly here and there through the rifts of the clouds. Holmes drove in silence, with his head sunk upon his breast, and the air of a man who is lost in thought, whilst I sat beside him, curious to learn what this new quest might be which seemed to tax his powers so sorely, and yet afraid to break in upon the current of his thoughts. We had driven several miles, and were beginning to get to the fringe of the belt of suburban villas, when he shook himself, shrugged his shoulders, and lit up his pipe with the air of a man who has satisfied himself that he is acting for the best.

'You have a grand gift of silence, Watson,' said he. 'It makes you quite invaluable as a companion. 'Pon my word, it is a great thing for me to have someone to talk to, for my own thoughts are not over pleasant. I was wondering what I should say to this dear little woman tonight when she meets me at the door.'

'You forget that I know nothing about it.'

'I shall just have time to tell you the facts of the case before we get to Lee. It seems absurdly simple, and yet, somehow, I can get nothing to go upon. There's plenty of thread, no doubt, but I can't get the end of it into my hand. Now, I'll state the case clearly and concisely to you, Watson, and maybe you may see a spark where all is dark to me.'

'Proceed then.'

'Some years ago – to be definite, in May, 1884 – there came to Lee a gentleman, Neville St Clair by name, who appeared to have plenty of money. He took a large villa, laid out the grounds very nicely, and lived generally in good style. By degrees he made friends in the neighbourhood, and in 1887 he married the daughter of a local brewer, by whom he has now had two children. He had no occupation, but was interested in several companies, and went into town as a rule in the morning, returning by the 5.14 from Cannon Street every night. Mr St Clair is now 37 years of age, is a man of temperate habits, a good husband, a very affectionate father, and a man who is popular with all who know him. I may add that his whole debts at the present moment, as far as we have been able to ascertain, amount to £88.10s., while he has £220 standing to his credit in the Capital and Counties Bank. There is no reason, therefore, to think that money troubles have been weighing upon his mind.

'Last Monday Mr Neville St Clair went into town rather earlier than usual, remarking before he started that he had two important commissions to perform, and that he would bring his little boy home a box of bricks. Now, by the merest chance his wife received a telegram upon this same Monday, very shortly after his departure, to the effect that a small parcel of considerable value which she had been expecting was waiting for her at the offices of the Aberdeen Shipping Company. Now, if you are well up in your London, you will know that the office of the company is in Fresno Street, which branches out of Upper Swandam Lane, where you found me tonight. Mrs St Clair had her lunch, started for the City, did some shopping, proceeded to the company's office, got her packet, and found herself exactly at 4.35 walking through Swandam Lane on her way back to the station. Have you followed me so far?'

'It is very clear.'

'If you remember, Monday was an exceedingly hot day, and Mrs St Clair walked slowly, glancing about in the hope of seeing a cab, as she did not like the neighbourhood in which she found herself. While she walked in this way down Swandam Lane she suddenly heard an ejaculation or cry, and was struck cold to see her husband looking down at her, and, as it seemed to her, beckoning to her from a second-floor window. The window was open, and she distinctly saw his face, which she describes as being terribly agitated. He waved his hands frantically to her, and then vanished from the window so suddenly that it seemed to her that he had been plucked back by some irresistible force from behind. One singular point which struck her quick feminine eye was that, although he wore some dark coat, such as he had started to town in, he had on neither collar nor necktie.

'Convinced that something was amiss with him, she rushed down the steps – for the house was none other than the opium den in which you found me tonight – and, running through the front room, she attempted to ascend the stairs which led to the first floor. At the foot of the stairs, however, she met this Lascar scoundrel of whom I have spoken, who thrust her back and, aided by a Dane, who acts as assistant there, pushed her out into the street. Filled with the most maddening doubts and fears, she rushed down the lane, and, by rare good fortune, met, in Fresno Street, a number of constables with an inspector, all on their way to their beat. The inspector and two men accompanied her back, and, in spite of the continued resistance of the proprietor, they made their way to the room in which Mr St Clair had last been seen. There was no sign of him there. In fact, in the whole of that floor there was no one to be found, save a crippled wretch of hideous aspect, who, it seems, made his home there. Both he and Lascar stoutly swore that no one else had been in the front room during that afternoon. So determined was their denial that the inspector was staggered, and had almost come to believe that Mrs St Clair had been deluded when, with a cry, she sprang at a small deal box which lay upon the table, and tore the lid from it. Out there fell a cascade of children's bricks. It was the toy which he had promised to bring home.

'This discovery, and the evident confusion which the cripple showed, made the inspector realize that the matter was serious. The rooms were carefully examined, and results all pointed to an abominable crime. The front room was plainly furnished as a sitting-room, and led into a small bedroom, which looked out upon the back of one of the wharves. Between the wharf and the bedroom window is a narrow strip, which is dry at low tide, but is covered at high tide with at least four and a half feet of water. The bedroom window was a broad one, and opened from below. On examination traces of blood were to be seen upon the window-sill, and several scattered drops were visible upon the wooden floor of the bedroom. Thrust away behind a curtain in the front room were all the clothes of Mr Neville St Clair, with the exception of his coat. His boots, his socks, his hat, and his watch – all were there. There were no signs of violence upon any of these garments, and there were no other traces of Mr Neville St Clair. Out of the window he must apparently have gone, for no other exit could be discovered, and the ominous bloodstains upon the sill gave little promise that he could save himself by swimming, for the tide was at its very highest at the moment of the tragedy.

'And now as to the villains who seemed to be immediately implicated in the matter. The Lascar was known to be a man of the vilest antecedents*, but as by Mrs St Clair's story he was known to have been at the foot of the stair within a very few seconds of her husband's appearance at the window, he could hardly have been more than an accessory to the crime. His defence was one of absolute ignorance, and he protested that he had no knowledge as to the doings of Hugh Boone, his lodger, and that he could not account in any way for the presence of the missing gentleman's clothes.

'So much for the Lascar manager. Now for the sinister cripple who lives upon the second floor of the opium den, and who was certainly the last human being whose eyes rested upon Neville St Clair. His name is Hugh Boone, and his hideous face is one which is familiar to every man who goes much to the City. He is a professional beggar, though in order to avoid the police regulations he pretends to a small trade in wax vestas*. Some little distance down Threadneedle Street upon the left hand side there is, as you may have remarked, a small angle in the wall. Here it is that the creature takes his daily seat, cross-legged, with his tiny stock of matches on his lap, and as he is a piteous spectacle a small rain of charity descends into the greasy leather cap which lies upon the pavement beside him. I have watched the fellow more than once, before ever I thought of making his professional acquaintance, and I have been surprised at the harvest which he has reaped in a short time. His appearance, you see, is so remarkable, that no one can pass him without observing him. A shock of orange hair, a pale face disfigured by a horrible scar, which, by its contraction, has turned up the outer edge of his upper lip, a bull-dog chin, and a pair of very penetrating dark eyes, which present a singular contrast to the colour of his hair, all mark him out from amid

---

*antecedents: background history
*wax vestas: matches

the common crowd of mendicants*, and so, too, does his wit, for he is ever ready with a reply to any piece of chaff which may be thrown at him by the passers-by. This is the man whom we now learn to have been the lodger at the opium den, and to have been the last man to see the gentleman of whom we are in quest.'

'But a cripple!' said I. 'What could he have done single-handed against a man in the prime of life?'

'He is a cripple in the sense that he walks with a limp; but, in other respects, he appears to be a powerful and well-nurtured man. Surely your medical experience would tell you, Watson, that weakness in one limb is often compensated for by exceptional strength in the others?'

'Pray continue your narrative.'

'Mrs St Clair had fainted at the sight of the blood upon the window, and she was escorted home in a cab by the police, as her presence could be of no help to them in their investigations. Inspector Barton, who had charge of the case, made a very careful examination of the premises, but without finding anything which threw any light upon the matter. One mistake had been made in not arresting Boone instantly, as he was allowed some few minutes during which he might have communicated with his friend Lascar, but this fault was soon remedied, and he was seized and searched, without anything being found which could incriminate him. There were, it is true, some bloodstains upon his right shirt-sleeve, but he pointed to his ring finger, which had been cut near the nail, and explained that the bleeding came from there, adding that he had been to the window not long before, and that the stains which had been observed there came doubtless from the same source. He denied strenuously having ever seen Mr Neville St Clair, and swore that the presence of the clothes in his room was as much a mystery to him as to the police. As to Mrs St Clair's assertion that she had actually seen her husband at the window, he declared that she must have been either mad or dreaming. He was removed, loudly protesting, to

---

*mendicants: beggars

the police station, while the inspector remained upon the premises in the hope that the ebbing tide might afford some fresh clue.

'And it did, though they hardly found upon the mudbank what they had feared to find. It was Neville St Clair's coat, and not Neville St Clair, which lay uncovered as the tide receded. And what do you think they found in the pockets?'

'I cannot imagine.'

'No, I don't think you will guess. Every pocket stuffed with pennies and half-pennies – four hundred and twenty-one pennies, and two hundred and seventy half-pennies. It was no wonder that it had not been swept away by the tide. But a human body is a different matter. There is a fierce eddy between the wharf and the house. It seemed likely enough that the weighted coat had remained when the stripped body had been sucked away into the river.'

'But I understand that all the other clothes were found in the room. Would the body be dressed in a coat alone?'

'No, sir, but the facts might be met speciously* enough. Suppose that this man Boone had thrust Neville St Clair through the window, there is no human eye which could have seen the deed. What would he do then? It would of course instantly strike him that he must get rid of the tell-tale garments. He would seize the coat then, and be in the act of throwing it out when it would occur to him that it would swim and not sink. He has little time, for he has heard the scuffle downstairs when the wife tried to force her way up, and perhaps he has already heard from his Lascar confederate that the police are hurrying up the street. There is not an instant to be lost. He rushes to some secret horde, where he has accumulated the fruits of his beggary, and he stuffs all the coins upon which he can lay his hands into the pockets to make sure of the coat's sinking. He throws it out, and would have done the same with the other garments had not he heard the rush of steps below, and only just had time to close the window when the police appeared.'

---

speciously: plausibly

'It certainly sounds feasible.'

'Well, we will take it as a working hypothesis for want of a better. Boone, as I have told you, was arrested and taken to the station, but it could not be shown that there had ever before been anything against him. He had for years been known as a professional beggar, but his life appeared to have been a very quiet and innocent one. There the matter stands at present, and the questions which have to be solved, what Neville St Clair was doing in the opium den, what happened to him when there, where is he now, and what Hugh Boone had to do with his disappearance, are all as far from solution as ever. I confess that I cannot recall any case within my experience which looked at the first glance so simple, and yet which presented such difficulties.'

Whilst Sherlock Holmes had been detailing this singular series of events we had been whirling through the outskirts of the great town until the last straggling houses had been left behind, and we rattled along with a country hedge upon either side of us. Just as he finished, however, we drove through two scattered villages, where a few lights still glimmered in the windows.

'We are on the outskirts of Lee,' said my companion. 'We have touched on three English counties in our short drive, starting in Middlesex, passing over an angle of Surrey, and ending in Kent. See that light among the trees? That is the Cedars, and beside that lamp sits a woman whose anxious ears have already, I have little doubt, caught the clink of our horses's feet.'

'But why are you not conducting the case from Baker Street?' I asked.

'Because there are many inquiries which must be made out here. Mrs St Clair has most kindly put two rooms at my disposal, and you may rest assured that she will have nothing but a welcome for my friend and colleague. I hate to meet her, Watson, when I have no news of her husband. Here we are. Whoa, there, whoa!'

We had pulled up in front of a large villa which stood within its own grounds. A stable-boy had run out to the horse's head, and, springing down, I followed Holmes up the small, winding gravel drive which led to the house. As we approached, the door flew open, and a little blonde woman stood in the opening, clad in some sort of light *mousseline de soie**, with a touch of fluffy pink chiffon at her neck and wrists. She stood with her figure outlined against the flood of light, one hand upon the door, one half raised in her eagerness, her body slightly bent, her head and face protruded, with eager eyes and parted lips, a standing question.

'Well?' she cried, 'well?' And then, seeing that there were two of us, she gave a cry of hope which sank into a groan as she saw that my companion shook his head and shrugged his shoulders.

'No good news?'

'None.'

'No bad?'

'No.'

'Thank God for that. But come in. You must be weary, for you have had a long day.'

'This is my friend, Dr Watson. He has been of most vital use to me in several of my cases, and a lucky chance has made it possible for me to bring him out and associate him with this investigation.'

'I am delighted to see you,' said she, pressing my hand warmly. 'You will, I am sure, forgive anything which may be wanting in our arrangements, when you consider the blow which has come so suddenly upon us.'

'My dear madam,' said I, 'I am an old campaigner, and if I were not, I can very well see that no apology is needed. If I can be of any assistance, either to you or to my friend here, I shall be indeed happy.'

'Now, Mr Sherlock Holmes,' said the lady, as we entered a well-lit dining-room, upon the table of which a cold supper had been laid out. 'I should very much like to ask you one or two plain questions, to which I beg you will give a plain answer.'

'Certainly, madam.'

---

**mousseline de soie*: silk muslin

'Do not trouble about my feelings. I am not hysterical, nor given to fainting. I simply wish to hear your real, real opinion.'

'Upon what point?'

'In your heart of hearts do you think that Neville is alive?'

Sherlock Holmes seemed to be embarrassed by the question. 'Frankly now!' she repeated, standing upon the rug, and looking keenly down at him, as he leaned back in a basket chair.

'Frankly then, madam, I do not.'

'You think that he is dead?'

'I do.'

'Murdered?'

'I don't say that. Perhaps.'

'And on what day did he meet his death?'

'On Monday.'

'Then perhaps, Mr Holmes, you will be good enough to explain how it is that I have received this letter from him today.'

Sherlock Holmes sprang out of his chair as if he had been galvanized*.

'What!' he roared.

'Yes, today.' She stood smiling, holding up a little slip of paper in the air.

'May I see it?'

'Certainly.'

He snatched it from her in his eagerness, and smoothing it out upon the table, he drew over the lamp, and examined it intently. I had left my chair, and was gazing at it over his shoulder. The envelope was a very coarse one, and was stamped with the Gravesend postmark, and with the date of that very day, or rather of the day before, for it was considerably after midnight.

'Coarse writing!' murmured Holmes. 'Surely this is not your husband's writing, madam.'

'No, but the enclosure is.'

'I perceive also that whoever addressed the envelope had to go and inquire as to the address.'

---

*galvanized: subjected to an electric shock

'How can you tell that?'

'The name, you see, is in perfectly black ink, which has dried itself. The rest is of the greyish colour which shows that blotting-paper has been used. If it had been written straight off, and then blotted, none would be of a deep black shade. This man has written the name, and there has then been a pause before he wrote the address, which can only mean that he was not familiar with it. It is, of course, a trifle, but there is nothing so important as trifles. Let us now see the letter! Ha! there has been an enclosure here!'

'Yes, there was a ring. His signet ring.'

'And you are sure that this is your husband's hand?'

'One of his hands.'

'One?'

'His hand when he wrote hurriedly. It is very unlike his usual writing, and yet I know it well.'

'"Dearest, do not be frightened. All will come well. There is a huge error which it may take some little time to rectify. Wait in patience – Neville." Written in pencil upon the fly-leaf of a book, octavo size, no watermark. Posted today in Gravesend by a man with a dirty thumb. Ha! And the flap has been gummed, if I am not very much in error, by a person who had been chewing tobacco. And you have no doubt that it is your husband's hand, madam?'

'None. Neville wrote those words.'

'And they were posted today at Gravesend. Well, Mrs St Clair, the clouds lighten, though I should not venture to say that the danger is over.'

'But he must be alive, Mr Holmes.'

'Unless this is a clever forgery to put us on the wrong scent. The ring, after all, proves nothing. It may have been taken from him.'

'No, no; it is, it is, it is his very own writing!'

'Very well. It may, however, have been written on Monday, and only posted today.'

'That is possible.'

'If so, much may have happened between.'

'Oh, you must not discourage me, Mr Holmes. I know that

all is well with him. There is so keen a sympathy between us that I should know if evil came upon him. On the very day that I saw him last he cut himself in the bedroom, and yet I in the dining-room rushed upstairs instantly with the utmost certainty that something had happened. Do you think that I would respond to such a trifle, and yet be ignorant of his death?'

'I have seen too much not to know that the impression of a woman may be more valuable than the conclusion of an analytical reasoner. And in this letter you certainly have a very strong piece of evidence to corroborate your view. But if your husband is alive and able to write letters, why should he remain away from you?'

'I cannot imagine. It is unthinkable.'

'And on Monday he made no remarks before leaving you?'

'No.'

''And you were surprised to see him in Swandam Lane?'

'Very much so.'

'Was the window open?'

'Yes.'

'Then he might have called to you?'

'He might.'

'He only, as I understand, gave an inarticulate cry?'

'Yes.'

'A call for help, you thought?'

'Yes. He waved his hands.'

'But it might have been a cry of surprise. Astonishment at the unexpected sight of you might cause him to throw up his hands?'

'It is possible.'

'And you thought he was pulled back.'

'He disappeared so suddenly.'

'He might have leapt back. You did not see anyone else in the room?'

'No, but this horrible man confessed to having been there, and the Lascar was at the foot of the stairs.'

'Quite so. Your husband, as far as you could see, had his ordinary clothes on?'

'But without his collar or tie. I distinctly saw his bare throat.'

'Had he ever spoken of Swandam Lane?'

'Never.'

'Had he ever shown any signs of having taken opium?'

'Never.'

'Thank you, Mrs St Clair. Those are the principal points about which I wished to be absolutely clear. We shall now have a little supper and then retire, for we may have a very busy day tomorrow.'

A large and comfortable double-bedded room had been placed at our disposal, and I was quickly between the sheets, for I was weary after my night of adventure. Sherlock Holmes was a man, however, who when he had an unsolved problem upon his mind would go for days, and even for a week, without rest, turning it over, rearranging his facts, looking at it from every point of view, until he had either fathomed it, or convinced himself that his data were insufficient. It was soon evident to me that he was now preparing for an all-night sitting. He took off his coat and waistcoat, put on a large blue dressing gown, and then wandered about the room collecting pillows from his bed, and cushions from the sofa and armchairs. With these he constructed a sort of Eastern divan, upon which he perched himself crosslegged, with an ounce of shag tobacco and a box of matches laid out in front of him. In the dim light of the lamp I saw him sitting there, an old brier pipe between his lips, his eyes fixed vacantly upon the corner of the ceiling, the blue smoke curling up from him, silent, motionless, with the light shining upon his strong set aquiline* features. So he sat as I dropped off to sleep, and so he sat when a sudden ejaculation caused me to wake up, and I found the summer sun shining into the apartment. The pipe was still between his lips, the smoke still curled upwards, and the room was full of a dense tobacco haze, but nothing remained of the heap of shag which I had seen upon the previous night.

'Awake, Watson?' he asked.

'Yes.'

'Game for a morning drive?'

---

aquiline: eagle-like

'Certainly.'

'Then dress. No one is stirring yet, but I know where the stable boy sleeps, and we shall soon have the trap out.' He chuckled to himself as he spoke, his eyes twinkled, and he seemed a different man to the sombre thinker of the previous night.

As I dressed I glanced at my watch. It was no wonder that no one was stirring. It was twenty-five minutes past four. I had hardly finished when Holmes returned with the news that the boy was putting in the horse.

'I want to test a little theory of mine,' said he, pulling on his boots. 'I think, Watson, that you are now standing in the presence of one of the most absolute fools in Europe. I deserve to be kicked from here to Charing Cross. But I think I have the key of the affair now.'

'And where is it?' I asked, smiling.

'In the bathroom,' he answered. 'Oh, yes, I am not joking,' he continued, seeing my look of incredulity. 'I have just been there, and I have taken it out, and I have got it in this Gladstone bag. Come on, my boy, and we shall see whether it will not fit the lock.'

We made our way downstairs as quietly as possible, and out into the bright morning sunshine. In the road stood our horse and trap, with the half-clad stable-boy waiting at the head. We both sprang in, and away we dashed down the London Road. A few country carts were stirring, bearing in vegetables to the metropolis, but the lines of villas on either side were as silent and lifeless as some city in a dream.

'It has been in some points a singular case,' said Holmes, flicking the horse on into a gallop. 'I confess that I have been as blind as a mole, but it is better to learn wisdom late, than never to learn it at all.'

In town, the earliest risers were just beginning to look sleepily from their windows as we drove through the streets of the Surrey side. Passing down the Waterloo Bridge Road we crossed over the river, and, dashing up Wellington Street, wheeled sharply to the right and found ourselves in Bow Street. Sherlock Holmes was well known to the Force, and the two constables at the door saluted him. One of them held the horse's head while the other led us in.

'Who is on duty?' asked Holmes.

'Inspector Bradstreet, sir.'

'Ah, Bradstreet, how are you?' A tall, stout official had come down the stone-flagged passage, in a peaked cap and frogged jacket. 'I wish to have a quiet word with you, Bradstreet.'

'Certainly, Mr Holmes. Step into my room here.'

It was a small office-like room, with a huge ledger upon the table, and a telephone projecting from the wall. The inspector sat down at his desk.

'What can I do for you, Mr Holmes?'

'I called about that beggar-man, Boone – the one who was charged with being concerned in the disappearance of Mr Neville St Clair, of Lee.'

'Yes. He was brought up and remanded for further inquiries.'

'So I heard. You have him here?'

'In the cells.'

'Is he quiet?'

'Oh, he gives no trouble. But he is a dirty scoundrel.'

'Dirty?'

'Yes, it is all we can do to make him wash his hands, and his face is as black as a tinker's. Well, when once his case has been settled he will have a regular prison bath; and I think, if you saw him, you would agree with me that he needed it.'

'I should like to see him very much.'

'Would you? That is easily done. Come this way. You can leave your bag.'

'No, I think I'll take it.'

'Very good. Come this way, if you please.' He led us down a passage, opened a barred door, passed down a winding stair, and brought us to a white-washed corridor with a line of doors on each side.

'The third on the right is his,' said the inspector. 'Here it is!' He quietly shot back a panel in the upper part of the door, and glanced through.

'He is asleep,' said he. 'You can see him very well.'

We both put our eyes to the grating. The prisoner lay with

his face towards us, in a very deep sleep, breathing slowly and heavily. He was a middle-sized man, coarsely clad as became his calling, with a coloured shirt protruding through the rent in his tattered coat. He was, as the inspector had said, extremely dirty, but the grime which covered his face could not conceal its repulsive ugliness. A broad weal from an old scar ran right across it from eye to chin, and by its contraction had turned up one side of the upper lip, so that three teeth were exposed in a perpetual snarl. A shock of very bright red hair grew low over his eyes and forehead.

'He's a beauty, isn't he?' said the inspector.

'He certainly needs a wash,' remarked Holmes. 'I had an idea that he might, and I took the liberty of bringing the tools with me.' He opened his Gladstone bag as he spoke, and took out, to my astonishment, a very large bath sponge.

'He! he! You are a funny one,' chuckled the inspector.

'Now, if you will have the great goodness to open that door very quietly, we will soon make him cut a much more respectable figure.'

'Well, I don't know why not,' said the inspector. 'He doesn't look a credit to the Bow Street cells, does he?' He slipped his key into the lock and we all very quietly entered the cell. The sleeper half turned, and then settled down once more into a deep slumber. Holmes stooped to the water jug, moistened his sponge, and then rubbed it twice vigorously across and down the prisoner's face.

'Let me introduce you,' he shouted, 'to Mr Neville St Clair, of Lee, in the county of Kent.'

Never in my life have I seen such a sight. The man's face peeled off under the sponge like the bark from a tree. Gone was the coarse brown tint! Gone, too, the horrid scar which had seamed it across, and the twisted lip which had given the repulsive sneer to the face! A twitch brought away the tangled red hair, and there, sitting up in his bed, was a pale, sad-faced, refined-looking man, black-haired and smooth-skinned, rubbing his eyes, and staring about him with sleepy bewilderment. Then suddenly realising the exposure, he broke into a scream, and threw himself down with his face to the pillow.

'Great heaven!' cried the inspector, 'it is, indeed, the missing man. I know him from the photograph.'

The prisoner turned with the reckless air of a man who abandons himself to his destiny. 'Be it so,' said he. 'And pray, what am I charged with.'

'With making away with Mr Neville St— Oh, come, you can't be charged with that, unless they make a case of attempted suicide of it,' said the inspector, with a grin. 'Well, I have been twenty-seven years in the force, but this really takes the cake.'

'If I am Mr Neville St Clair, then it is obvious that no crime has been committed, and that, therefore, I am illegally detained.'

'No crime, but a very great error has been committed,' said Holmes. 'You would have done better to have trusted your wife.'

'It was not the wife, it was the children,' groaned the prisoner. 'God help me, I would not have them ashamed of their father. My God! What an exposure! What can I do?'

Sherlock Holmes sat down beside him on the couch, and patted him kindly on the shoulder.

'If you leave it to a court of law to clear the matter up,' said he, 'of course you can hardly avoid publicity. On the other hand, if you convince the police authorities that there is no possible case against you, I do not know that there is any reason that the details should find their way into the papers. Inspector Bradstreet would, I am sure, make notes upon anything which you might tell us, and submit it to the proper authorities. The case would then never go into court at all.'

'God bless you!' cried the prisoner, passionately. 'I would have endured imprisonment, aye, even execution, rather than have left my miserable secret as a family blot to my children.

'You are the first who have ever heard my story. My father was a schoolmaster in Chesterfield, where I received an excellent education. I travelled in my youth, took to the stage, and finally became a reporter on an evening paper in London. One day my editor wished to have a series of articles upon begging in the metropolis, and I volunteered to supply them. There was the point from which all my adventures started. It was only by trying begging as an amateur that I could get the facts upon which to base my articles. When an actor I had, of course, learned all the secrets of making up, and had been famous in the green-room* for my skill. I took advantage now of my attainments. I painted my face, and to make myself as pitiable as possible I made a good scar and fixed one side of my lip in a twist by the aid of a small slip of flesh-coloured plaster. Then with a red head of hair, and an appropriate dress, I took my station in the busiest part of the City, ostensibly as a match-seller, but really as a beggar. For seven hours I plied my trade, and when I returned home in the evening I found, to my surprise, that I had received no less than twenty-six shillings and fourpence.

'I wrote my articles, and thought little more of the matter until, some time later, I backed a bill for a friend, and had a writ served upon me for £25. I was at my wits' end where to get the money, but a sudden idea came to me. I begged a fortnight's grace from the creditor, asked for a holiday from my employers, and spent the time in begging in the City under my disguise. In ten days I had the money, and had paid the debt.

'Well, you can imagine how hard it was to settle down to arduous work at two pounds a week, when I knew that I could earn as much in a day by smearing my face with a little paint, laying my cap on the ground, and sitting still. It was a long fight between my pride and the money, but the dollars won at last, and I threw up reporting, and sat day after day in the corner which I had first chosen, inspiring pity by my ghastly face, and filling my pockets with coppers. Only one man knew my secret. He was the keeper of a low den in which I used to lodge in Swandam Lane, where I could every morning emerge as a squalid beggar, and in the evenings transform myself into a well-dressed man about town. This fellow, a Lascar, was well paid by me for his rooms, so that I knew that my secret was safe in his possession.

---

*green-room: actors' rest-room in a theatre

'Well, very soon I found that I was saving considerable sums of money. I do not mean that any beggar in the streets of London could earn seven hundred pounds a year – which is less than my average takings – but I had exceptional advantages in my power of making up, and also in a facility in repartee, which improved by practice, and made me quite a recognized character in the City. All day a stream of pennies, varied by silver, poured in upon me, and it was a very bad day upon which I failed to take two pounds.

'As I grew richer I grew more ambitious, took a house in the country, and eventually married, without anyone having a suspicion as to my real occupation. My dear wife knew that I had business in the City. She little knew what.

'Last Monday I had finished for the day, and was dressing in my room above the opium den, when I looked out of the window, and saw, to my horror and astonishment, that my wife was standing in the street, with her eyes fixed full upon me. I gave a cry of surprise, threw up my arms to cover my face, and rushing to my confidant, the Lascar, entreated him to prevent anyone from coming up to me. I heard her voice downstairs, but I knew that she could not ascend. Swiftly I threw off my clothes, pulled on those of a beggar, and put on my pigments and wig. Even a wife's eyes could not pierce so complete a disguise. But then it occurred to me that there might be a search in the room and that the clothes might betray me. I threw open the window, re-opening by my violence a small cut which I had inflicted upon myself in the bedroom that morning. Then I seized my coat, which was weighted by the coppers which I had just transferred to it from the leather bag in which I carried my takings. I hurled it out of the window, and it disappeared into the Thames. The other clothes would have followed, but at that moment there was a rush of constables up the stairs, and a few minutes after I found, rather, I confess, to my relief, that instead of being identified as Mr Neville St Clair, I was arrested as his murderer.

'I do not know that there is anything else for me to explain. I was determined to preserve my disguise as long as possible, and hence my preference for a dirty face. Knowing that my wife would be terribly anxious, I slipped off my ring, and confided it to the Lascar at a moment when no constable was watching me, together with a hurried scrawl, telling her that she had no cause to fear.'

'That note only reached her yesterday,' said Holmes.

'Good God! What a week she must have spent.'

'The police have watched this Lascar,' said Inspector Bradstreet, 'and I can quite understand that he might find it difficult to post a letter unobserved. Probably he handed it to some sailor customer of his, who forgot all about it for some days.'

'That was it,' said Holmes, nodding approvingly, 'I have no doubt of it. But have you never been prosecuted for begging?'

'Many times; but what was a fine to me?'

'It must stop here, however,' said Bradstreet. 'If the police are to hush this thing up, there must be no more of Hugh Boone.'

'I have sworn it by the most solemn oaths which a man can take.'

'In that case I think that it is probable that no further steps may be taken. But if you are found again, then all must come out. I am sure, Mr Holmes, that we are very much indebted to you for having cleared the matter up. I wish I knew how you reach your results.'

'I reached this one,' said my friend, 'by sitting upon five pillows and consuming an ounce of shag. I think, Watson, that if we drive to Baker Street we shall just be in time for breakfast.'

# The Lieabout
## Margery Allingham

Like *The Man with the Twisted Lip*, this story is set in the city, but here the city is a place 'of surprising intimacy and friendliness'. The narrator of the story is a woman going about her daily business of shopping and walking the dog. When she strikes up an acquaintance with a tramp, the 'lieabout', we are left in no doubt about the social gulf which divides them. Her precise and polite language is set against the rough and ready appearance and language of the tramp. She describes, with a bemused detachment, the unfolding drama of the crime, but we soon realize that the narrator herself has been tricked.

**Margery Allingham** (1904–1966) published her first novel when she was seventeen. She published thirty novels in all, twenty-one of them featuring the fictional detective Albert Campion. *The Lieabout* is from *The Allingham Casebook*, a collection of her short stories first published in the 1930s.

I still have the brooch but I can hardly wear it. I thought of throwing it away once, but it is so very pretty. I don't think it is valuable but I have never dared to take it into a jeweller's to find out. It is a very awkward position.

I might have sent it back to the people who owned it, in fact I ought to have done that, but if ever it was traced to me who would believe my story?

It was when we lived in London. We had a small flat in a courtyard leading off High Holborn, right in the city. The courtyard was really only the foot of an air-shaft striking down amid enormous office buildings. There were only two doors in it; one belonged to a printing works and the other one was ours.

When you opened our door you found yourself at the foot of a flight of steep stairs, at the top of which were our three rooms and a sort of corridor called a kitchenette-bath.

Our domain had once been the caretaker's premises of the insurance building which was below us and still ran right through to the main street. By the time we went there it had been converted into two shops. These shops were empty when we arrived and remained so for nearly a year, although from time to time gangs of workmen were very busy in them, obliterating, we supposed, still more of the atmosphere of insurance.

There are several odd things about living in the city. One is the quiet of the place at night. When we moved to the country the noises of the night birds were almost too much for us after that deathly peace of the City of London when the offices have closed.

Another curious thing is the surprising intimacy and friendliness of it all. In no village in which I ever lived did I acquire so many acquaintances.

The shops where one could buy the ordinary necessities of life as opposed to an adding machine, a battleship or a two-thousand-guinea emerald ring were all of the small and homely variety and were nearly all of them tucked away in courtyards like our own. The people who owned them were friendly and obliging and told us their family histories at the slightest encouragement.

The news-sellers and the hawkers were other regulars who were anxious to gossip or pass the time of day, and as I walked down the crowded pavement with my shopping basket on my arm I found I had as many people to nod to as if I were in a small town street which had suddenly become overrun with half a million foreigners.

I first met the Lieabout in our own yard. He was sitting there one evening among a pile of packing-cases from the printing works when I went out to play with Addlepate. Addlepate leapt on him, mistaking him for a sack of waste paper in which he delighted. The misapprehension led to a sort of introduction and after a while the Lieabout watched the dog to see that he did not go out into the traffic and commit suicide and I went up to get the man some tea.

He was a frail old person with a beaky face and little bright red eyes like a ferret or one of the old black rats who come out and dance on the cobbles in the small hours.

All lieabouts are necessarily dirty. Genuine tramping can never be a hygienic method of life. But he was horribly so. He looked as though he had just slipped down from his niche among the gargoyles of St Paul's before the cleaners could get him. He was sooty with London, and his garments, which were varied and of dubious origin, were all the same grey-black colour, and not with dye.

He was glad of the tea, and when I said I had not seen him about before, he explained that he had come up from Cheapside, where he had been spending the summer. He did not ask for money and I did not offer him any, naturally. We parted friends, he to return to his packing-cases in which he was making himself a temporary home and I to my work upstairs.

He lived in the packing-cases for nearly a week and we kept up a nodding acquaintance.

I was out shopping one morning when I saw the brooch. It was on a lower shelf in the window of one of those very big jewellers and silversmiths whose principal trade seems to be in challenge cups and presentation plate. The shop was not quite opposite the entrance to our courtyard but about fifty yards down on the other side of the traffic. I stood for some time looking at the brooch. It consisted of seven large topaz set in oxydised silver and the finished effect was rather like the rose window in Notre Dame.

I was still gazing at it when the Lieabout appeared at my elbow.

'Nice, ain't it? he said. 'Goin' to 'ave it?'

I laughed and indicated my basket, which held one of Addlepate's Friday bones protruding rather disgustingly from a sea of lettuce.

'Not this week. Food's gone up,' I said, and would have passed on, but the ornament had evidently attracted him, too, for he came nearer to look at it and I should have had to brush past him to get into the jostling stream in the middle of the pavement again.

'It's not worfa thousand quid,' he observed, after a moment

or so of contemplation. 'Go in an' arsk 'em. They'll say a tenner, I betcha.'

'Very likely,' I said. 'And what should I do?'

He grinned at me, disclosing a most disreputable assortment of different-size teeth.

'Same as me, I reckon,' he said. 'Beat it like one o'clock. 'Day, lady.'

I went home and forgot all about the incident and the next day was Saturday.

Up to this point the story was quite ordinary, but once the police came into it the whole thing became a little fantastic.

Saturday morning in the city always has a last day at boarding school atmosphere. Fewer strangers swoop out of the fat red buses or come boiling up out of the tubes, and those that do appear are definitely in holiday mood. When the big clock of St Paul's strikes noon the exodus begins, and by a quarter to one the streets look like a theatre after the show is over.

The road outside our courtyard, which all the week had been a sort of nightmare Brooklands*, turned suddenly into a great river of dull glass, with only an occasional bus or taxi speeding happily down its wide expanse.

There were people about, of course, but only a dozen or so, and the city policemen in their enormous helmets, which they use as personal suitcases, I believe, stood out, lonely and important.

It was nearly two o'clock on this particular Saturday afternoon when the police arrived. My husband leant out of the studio window and reported that there were two large bobbies on the step. I went down to open the door. None of our visitors had left a car outside the yard gates for some considerable time, but although my conscience was clear, much clearer than it is now, I felt vaguely uneasy. One policeman may be a friend, but two are the Law.

Oh the step I found two of the largest, bluest specimens I have ever seen, and they were both vastly uncomfortable. They hesitated, eyeing first me and then each other with embarrassment.

---

*Brooklands: pre-war motor racing circuit

I waited awkwardly for them to begin, and presently the larger one spoke.

'I wonder if you'd do me a personal favour, Ma'am?' he said.

It was such an unexpected request that I gaped at him, and he continued:

'I want you to go out into the street and look in the empty shop next door. Don't say nothing to anyone. Just behave perfectly casual, and then come back and tell us what you think you see.'

I began to feel a trifle lightheaded, but they were certainly real policemen and, anyway, Addlepate was barking his head off at the top of the stairs.

'All right,' I said stupidly. 'Aren't you coming?'

The other constable shook his head.

'No, Ma'am. We don't want a crowd to collect. That's our idea. See?'

I went off obediently, and as soon as I turned out of the yard I saw that any hopes my official friends might have cherished concerning the absence of a crowd were doomed to disappointment. Everyone in the street seemed to be converging on the first of the empty shops, and I saw another policeman hurrying down the road towards the excitement.

On the step of the shop stood my friend the Lieabout. He was making a tremendous noise.

'It's a disgrice!' he was shouting. 'A bloomin' disgrice! It's bin there five days to my knowledge. Look at it. Look at it!'

I peered in through the plate glass and suddenly saw what he meant. The sight made me feel slightly sick. At the back of the shop was an archway leading into a further salon, which was lit by a skylight. All kinds of decorators' debris was strewn around, but among the whitewash pails, the planks and the trestles, was something covered with an old coat and a lump of sacking. The shape was suggestive. But the thing that made it horrible was the boot. The boot stuck out from beneath the coat so naturally and yet so lifelessly.

'It's a corp!' shrieked the Lieabout, to the crowd which had just reached us. 'A corp! Bin there five days. The p'lice won't do nothink. It's a murder, that's wot it is. A murdered corp!'

He turned to me.

'What are you waitin' for lady? Go and tell the rozzers it's a corp.'

His voice in my ear recalled me to my senses and I hurried back to my visitors. They were polite but impatient when I gave them my opinion, and it suddenly dawned upon me why I had been singled out for their confidence. A police officer is not allowed to enter private property without authority, nor do the regulations let him ask the owners of such property for permission to enter. But once he is invited in, and has a witness to prove it, he can go wherever his good sense tells him his duty lies.

'If you get out of our bedroom window on to the roof at the back of the shop you could look through the skylight,' I said. 'Would you care to?'

They were upstairs in an instant, and I had barely time to explain to my astonished husband before they were in the bedroom, negotiating the window. I say 'negotiating' because their climb through it required finesse, and a delicacy one would hardly have expected in men of their bulk.

It was one of those awkward old-fashioned sliding casements which permit a space about two and a half feet by one and a quarter when opened to their fullest extent.

It took a little time but out they went at last, helmets and all, and my husband with them. They disappeared over the roofs, and I was left to await their return.

However, by this time an entirely unsuspected bloodlust had taken possession of me and, unable to control my impatience where I was, I trotted down into the yard again and out into the street.

To be honest, I did not reach the street. The crowd was packed solid across our entrance, all straining and jostling to peer into the window of the shop next door.

I climbed up on the iron gate which closed the yard at night, and saw over the people's heads a great expanse of empty street to the east, while the west was packed with every vehicle which had passed that way since the Lieabout's sensational find.

It was because I was prevented by the angle of the wall from seeing my two police friends descending into the shop through the skylight that I was an exception from the rest of the crowd, and did not have my attention diverted from the excitement over the way.

I saw the long black car pull up outside the jeweller's shop and I saw the three men spring out of it. It was not until the crash of broken glass reached me, as the brick went through the window, that I realized that anything untoward was afoot.

The rest happened so quickly that I hardly followed it. I had a confused impression of flying figures, something flashing in the autumn sun and then of the black car sliding round like a speedboat in the broad road and flying away with smooth acceleration. In a moment it had gone completely. I could not even see which way it turned at the end of the street. Nothing but the ragged hole in the window, with a scared assistant's face peering through it, remained to show that the raid had occurred.

At that moment the first policeman to get down into the empty shop must have pulled away the coat, revealed the neatly arranged sacks and distemper tins beneath, and kicked the old boot away angrily, for the crowd suddenly became aware of the other sensation, and surged off across the road to gape anew.

It was extraordinarily neat. The whole thing had been done in one of the most important streets without anyone being able to give a clear picture of any of the men involved.

We heard all about the robbery from the tobacconist on the corner.

Ten thousand pounds' worth of valuables had been snatched, he said, including the gold state salt-cellar which an ancient and worshipful company was presenting to a foreign royal bridegroom, and which had been on view there for a few privileged days. A little small stuff went, too, he said; a couple of trays of rings and several oddments.

I never saw the Lieabout again. Foolishly I supposed that, after making such an ass of himself by his false alarm, he did not care to show his face in the neighbourhood and had moved off to another corner of the town.

The parcel came a week later. I found it in the letter box one night when we came in from a show.

It was the topaz brooch. It lay upon a mat of cottonwool, and there was a note with it written in a neat, educated hand. The message was brief and only too enlightening.

'Very many thanks for your valuable assistance,' it ran. 'Congratulate you. Very gratefully yours.'

There was no signature and the package had not been through the post.

So you see the problem: What should Mrs A. do now?

# Forever After
## Jim Thompson

This story is in strong contrast to the stories by Conan Doyle and Allingham. Whereas they concern themselves with a gentlemanly or ladylike sleuth viewing the scene of crime from a certain distance, *Forever After* takes the reader straight to the action in a direct and forceful way. Within the first two paragraphs the crime, criminals and motive are all set out in an urgent and uncompromising style.

Told in the third person, *Forever After* is a story of desire, passion and crime with multiple twists and turns which take the reader in totally unexpected directions. In doing so, the story pushes against the boundaries of the genre in a shocking yet satisfying way. With its brutal style, sense of fear and forceful dialogue, this story is an example of the American 'hard-boiled' school of detective fiction. Far away from the genteel drawing-rooms of much English detective fiction, this story deals with the often brutal consequences of crime.

**Jim Thompson** (1906–1977) wrote many examples of hard-boiled detective crime fiction such as *Savage Nights*, *The Killer Inside Me* and *A Hell of a Woman*. His heroes are often starkly unheroic, and their motives can verge on the psychopathic, with hints of their madness being revealed only gradually. His novel *The Grifters* was adapted by Stephen Frears into a successful film in 1990. The story *Forever After* was first published in 1960.

It was a few minutes before five o'clock when Ardis Clinton unlocked the rear door of her apartment, and admitted her lover. He was a cow-eyed young man with a wild mass of curly black hair. He worked as a dishwasher at Joe's Diner, which was directly across the alley.

They embraced passionately. Her body pressed against the meat cleaver, concealed inside his shirt, and Ardis shivered with delicious anticipation. Very soon now, it would all be over. That stupid ox, her husband, would be dead. He and his stupid cracks – all the dullness and boredom would be gone forever. And with the twenty thousand insurance money, ten thousand dollars double-indemnity ...

'We're going to be so happy, Tony,' she whispered. 'You'll have your own place, a real swank little restaurant with what they call one of those intimate bars. And you'll just manage it, just kind of saunter around in a dress suit, and –'

'And we'll live happily ever after,' Tony said. 'Just me and you, baby, walking down life's highway together.'

Ardis let out a gasp. She shoved him away from her, glaring up into his handsome empty face. 'Don't!' she snapped. 'Don't say things like that! I've told you and told you not to do it, and if I have to tell you again, I'll–!'

'But what'd I say?' he protested. 'I didn't say nothin'.'

'Well ...' She got control of herself, forcing a smile. 'Never mind, darling. You haven't had any opportunities and we've never really had a chance to know each other, so – so never mind. Things will be different after we're married.' She patted his cheek, kissed him again. 'You got away from the diner, all right? No one saw you leave?'

'Huh-uh. I already took the stuff up to the steam-table for Joe, and the waitress was up front too, y'know, filling the sugar bowls and the salt and pepper shakers like she always does just before dinner. And –'

'Good. Now, suppose someone comes back to the kitchen and finds out you're not there. What's your story going to be?'

'Well ... I was out in the alley dumping some garbage. I mean –' he corrected himself hastily, 'maybe I was. Or maybe I was down in the basement, getting some supplies. Or maybe I was in the john – the lavatory, I mean – or –'

'Fine,' Ardis said approvingly. 'You don't say where you were, so they can't prove you weren't there. You just don't remember where you were, understand, darling? You might have been any number of places.'

Tony nodded. Looking over her shoulder into the bedroom, he frowned worriedly. 'Why'd you do that now, honey? I know this has got to look like a robbery. But tearin' up the room now, before he gets here –'

'There won't be time afterwards. Don't worry, Tony. I'll keep the door closed.'

'But he might open it and look in. And if he sees all them dresser drawers dumped around, and –'

'He won't. He won't look into the bedroom. I know exactly what he'll do, exactly what he'll say, the same things that he's always done and said ever since we've been married. All the stupid, maddening, dull, tiresome – !' She broke off abruptly, conscious that her voice was rising. 'Well, forget it,' she said, forcing another smile. 'He won't give us any trouble.'

'Whatever you say,' Tony nodded docilely. 'If you say so, that's the way it is, Ardis.'

'But there'll be trouble – from the cops. I know I've already warned you about it, darling. But it'll be pretty bad, worse than anything you've ever gone through. They won't have any proof, but they're bound to be suspicious, and if you ever start talking, admitting anything –'

'I won't. They won't get anything out of me.'

'You're sure? They'll try to trick you. They'll probably tell you that I've confessed. They may even slap you around. So if you're not absolutely sure …'

'They won't get anything out of me,' he repeated stolidly. 'I won't talk.'

And studying him, Ardis knew that he wouldn't.

She led the way down the hall to the bathroom. He parted the shower curtains, and stepped into the tub. Drawing a pair of gloves from his pocket, he pulled them on to his hands. Awkwardly, he fumbled the meat cleaver from beneath his shirt.

'Ardis. Uh – look, honey.'

'Yes?'

'Do I have to hit you? Couldn't I just maybe give you a little shove, or –'

'No, darling,' she said gently. 'You have to hit me. This is supposed to be a robbery. If you killed my husband without doing anything to me, well, you know how it would look.'

'But I never hit no woman – any woman – before. I might hit you too hard, and –'

'Tony!'

'Well, all right,' he said sullenly. 'I don't like it, but all right.'

Ardis murmured soothing endearments. Then, brushing his lips quickly with her own, she returned to the living room. It was a quarter after five, exactly five minutes – but *exactly* – until her husband, Bill, would come home. Closing the bedroom door, she lay down on the lounge. Her negligee fell open, and she left it that way, grinning meanly as she studied the curving length of her thighs.

*Give the dope a treat for a change, she thought. Let him get one last good look before he gets his.*

Her expression changed. Wearily, resentfully, she pulled the material of the negligee over her legs. Because, of course, Bill would never notice. She could wear a ring in her nose, paint a bull's-eye around her navel, and he'd never notice.

If he had ever noticed, just once paid her a pretty compliment ...

If he had ever done anything different, ever said or done anything different at all – even the teensiest little bit ...

But he hadn't. Maybe he couldn't. So what else could she do but what she was doing? She could get a divorce, sure, but that was all she'd get. No money; nothing with which to build a new life. Nothing to make up for those fifteen years of slowly being driven mad.

*It's his own fault, she thought bitterly. I can't take any more. If I had to put up with him for just one more night, even one more hour ... !'*

She heard heavy footsteps in the hallway. Then, a key turned in the doorlatch, and Bill came in. He was a master machinist, a solidly built man of about forty-five. The old-fashioned gold-rimmed glasses on his pudgy nose gave him a look of owlish solemnity.

'Well,' he said, setting down his lunch bucket. 'Another day, another dollar.'

Ardis grimaced. He plodded across to the lounge, stooped, and gave her a half-hearted peck on the cheek.

'Long time no see,' he said. 'What we havin' for supper?'

Ardis gritted her teeth. It shouldn't matter, now; in a few minutes it would all be over. Yet somehow it *did* matter. He was as maddening to her as he had ever been.

'Bill …' She managed a seductive smile, slowly drawing the negligee apart. 'How do I look, Bill?'

'Okay,' he yawned. 'Got a little hole in your drawers, though. What'd you say we was havin' for supper?'

'Slop,' she said. 'Garbage. Trash salad with dirt dressing.'

'Sounds good. We got any hot water?'

Ardis sucked in her breath. She let it out again in a kind of infuriated moan. 'Of course, we've got hot water! Don't we always have? Well, don't we? Why do you have to ask every night?'

'So what's to get excited about?' he shrugged. 'Well, guess I'll go splash the chassis.'

He plodded off down the hall. Ardis heard the bathroom door open, and close. She got up, stood waiting by the telephone. The door banged open again, and Tony came racing up the hall.

He had washed off the cleaver. While he hastily tucked it back inside his shirt, Ardis dialled the operator. 'Help' she cried weakly. 'Help … police … murder!'

She let the receiver drop to the floor, spoke to Tony in a whisper. 'He's dead? You're sure of it?'

'Yeah, yeah, sure I'm sure. What do you think?'

'All right. Now, there's just one more thing …'

'I can't, Ardis. I don't want to. I –'

'Hit me,' she commanded, and thrust out her chin. 'Tony, I said to hit me!'

He hit her. A thousand stars blazed through her brain, and disappeared. And she crumpled silently to the floor.

…When she regained consciousness, she was lying on the lounge. A heavy-set man, a detective obviously, was seated at her side, and a white-jacketed young man with a stethoscope draped around his neck hovered nearby.

She had never felt better in her life. Even the lower part of her face, where Tony had smashed her, was surprisingly free of pain. Still, because it was what she should do, she moaned softly; spoke in a weak, hazy voice.

'Where am I? she said. 'What happened?'

'Lieutenant Powers,' the detective said. 'Suppose you tell me what happened, Mrs Clinton.'

'I ... I don't remember. I mean, well, my husband had just come home, and gone back to the bathroom. And there was a knock on the door, and I supposed it was the paper-boy or someone like that. So –'

'You opened the door and he rushed in and slugged you, right? Then what happened?'

'Well, then he rushed into the bedroom and started searching it. Yanking out the dresser drawers, and –'

'What was he searching for, Mrs Clinton? You don't have any considerable amount of money around, do you? Or any jewellery aside from what you're wearing? And it wasn't your husband's payday, was it?'

'Well, no. But –'

'Yes?'

'I don't know. Maybe he was crazy. All I know is what he did.'

'I see. He must have made quite a racket, seems to me. How come your husband didn't hear it?'

'He couldn't have. He had the shower running, and –'

She caught herself, fear constricting her throat. Lieutenant Powers grinned grimly.

'Missed a bet, huh, Mrs Clinton?'

'I – I don't know what you're –'

'Come off of it! The bathtub's dry as an oven. The shower was never turned on, and you know why it wasn't. Because there was a guy standing inside of it.'

'B-but – I don't know anything. I was unconscious, and –'

'Then, how do you know what happened? How do you know this guy went into the bedroom and started tearing it apart? And how did you make that telephone call?'

'Well, I ... I wasn't completely unconscious. I sort of knew what was going on without really –'

'Now, you listen to me,' he said harshly. 'You made that fake call of yours – yes, I said *fake* – to the operator at twenty-three minutes after five. There happened to be a prowl car right here in the neighbourhood, so two minutes later, at five-twenty-five, there were cops here in your apartment. You were unconscious then, more than an hour ago. You've been unconscious until just now.'

Ardis' brain whirled. Then, it cleared suddenly, and a great calm came over her.

'I don't see quite what you're hinting at, lieutenant. If you're saying that I was confused, mixed up – that I must have dreamed or imagined some of the things I told you – I'll admit it.'

'You know what I'm saying! I'm saying that no guy could have got in and out of this place, and done what this one did, in any two minutes!'

'Then the telephone operator must have been mistaken about the time,' Ardis said brightly. 'I don't know how else to explain it.'

Powers grunted. He said he could give her a better explanation – and he gave it to her. The right one. Ardis listened to it placidly, murmuring polite objections.

'That's ridiculous, lieutenant. Regardless of any gossip you may have heard, I don't know this, uh, Tony person. And I most certainly did not plot with him or anyone else to kill my husband. Why –'

'He says you did. We got a signed confession from him.'

'Have you?' But of course they didn't have. They might have found out about Tony, but he would never have talked. 'That hardly proves anything, does it?'

'Now, you listen to me, Mrs Clinton! Maybe you think that –'

'How is my husband, anyway? I do hope he wasn't seriously hurt.'

'How *is* he?' the lieutenant snarled. 'How would he be after gettin' worked over with –' He broke off, his eyes flickering. 'As a matter of fact,' he said heavily, 'he's going to be all right. He was pretty badly injured, but he was able to give us a statement and –'

'I'm so glad. But why are you questioning me, then?' It was another trick. Bill had to be dead. 'If he gave you a statement, then you must know that everything happened just like I said.'

She waited, looked at him quizzically. Powers scowled, his stern face wrinkling with exasperation.

'All right,' he said, at last. 'All right, Mrs Clinton. Your husband is dead. We don't have any statement from him, and we don't have any confession from Tony.'

'Yes?'

'But we know you're guilty, and you know that you are. And you'd better get if off your conscience while you still can.'

'While I still can?'

'Doc' – Powers jerked his head at the doctor. At the man, that is, who appeared to be a doctor. 'Lay it on the line, doc. Tell her that her boy friend hit her a little too hard.'

The man came forward hesitantly. He said, 'I'm sorry, Mrs Clinton. You have a – uh – you've sustained a very serious injury.'

'Have I?' Ardis smiled. 'I feel fine.'

'I don't think,' the doctor said judiciously, 'that that's quite true. What you mean is that you don't feel anything at all. You couldn't. You see, with an injury such as yours –'

'Get out,' Ardis said. 'Both of you get out.'

'Please, Mrs Clinton. Believe me, this isn't a trick. I haven't wanted to alarm you, but –'

'And you haven't,' she said. 'You haven't scared me even a little bit, mister. Now, clear out!'

She closed her eyes, kept them closed firmly. When, at last, she reopened them, Powers and the doctor – if he really had been a doctor – were gone. And the room was in darkness.

She lay smiling to herself, congratulating herself. In the corridor outside, she heard heavy footsteps approaching; and she tensed for a moment. Then, remembering, she relaxed again.

Not Bill, of course. She was through with that jerk forever. He'd driven her half out of her mind, got her to the point where she couldn't have taken another minute of him if her life depended on it. But now …

The footsteps stopped in front of her door. A key turned in the lock, the door opened and closed.

There was a clatter of a lunchpail being set down; then a familiar voice – maddeningly familiar words:

'Well. Another day, another dollar.'

Ardis' mouth tightened; it twisted slowly, in a malicious grin. So they hadn't given up yet! They were pulling this one last trick. Well, let them; she'd play along with the gag.

The man plodded across the room, stooped, and gave her a half-hearted peck on the cheek. 'Long time no see,' he said. 'What we havin' for supper?'

'Bill ...' Ardis said. 'How do I look, Bill?'

'Okay. Got your lipstick smeared, though. What'd you say we was having for supper?'

'Stewed owls! Now look, mister. I don't know who you –'

'Sounds good. We got any hot water?'

'Of course, we've got hot water! Don't we always have? Why do you always have to ask if – if –'

She couldn't go through with it. Even as a gag – even someone who merely sounded and acted like he did – it was too much to bear.

'Y-you get out of here!' she quavered. 'I don't have to stand for this! I *c-can't* stand it! I did it for fifteen years, and –'

'So what's to get excited about?' he said. 'Well, guess I'll go splash the chassis.'

'Stop it! *STOP IT*!' Her screams filled the room ... silent screams ripping through silence. 'He's – you're dead! I know you are! You're dead, and I don't have to put up with you for another minute. And – and – !'

'Wouldn't take no bets on that if I was you,' he said mildly. 'Not with a broken neck like yours.'

He trudged off toward the bathroom, wherever the bathroom is in Eternity.

# Crime and Detection: Activities

## 1 Comparing stories for wide reading

Compare and contrast the nature of the crime and its detection in *The Man with the Twisted Lip* by Sir Arthur Conan Doyle and
**either**
*The Lieabout* by Margery Allingham
**or**
*Forever After* by Jim Thompson

You might like to comment on:

- The different openings and how these generate atmosphere.
- The contrasting settings and the effect these have on the story.
- The trail of clues and red herrings left for the reader.
- The nature of the crime.
- How a feeling of menace and fear is generated.
- The contrasting styles of storytelling and use of language.
- The 'sting in the tail' – the way the endings set out to surprise.
- How these stories reflect the moral concerns of their day.

## 2 Opportunities for original writing

After reflecting on what you have learned from studying the stories in this section choose from one of the following:

- Write the opening of a detective story. Establish the setting, the crime and the characters involved.
- Write a description of contemporary city streets which will generate a sense of fear and unease in the reader.
- Write a crime story with the brutal style, sense of fear and hard-edged dialogue of a Jim Thompson 'hard-boiled' original.
- Tell a story with a trail of clues designed to confuse. Finish with an unexpected ending.

# Section 3
# Love

Without love where would we be? Babies and children need the love of a family to grow and thrive. We need the care and loyalty of friends at every stage in life. A loving relationship can bring a new intensity and fulfilment to our lives.The words that we use to describe love indicate just what a powerful emotion it is. We 'fall' in love – implying that this is something outside our control. The heart, which keeps us alive, is used as the symbol of love. We describe someone who evokes a passionate feeling as a 'heart-throb' and of course, when a relationship ends we are said to be 'heartbroken', as though life itself may not continue

Although love is a human condition which people have always experienced over the centuries, the expression of that love is strictly limited by the rules and culture of the period. People have not always been free to fall in love with anyone they chose, but have been restricted by considerations of social class, money, family and religion. Women's behaviour in particular has been governed by strict social conventions. In Victorian Britain women were not expected to feel strong passion, could never ask a man to marry them and were expected, in polite society, to remain a virgin until marriage.

As you read the following three love stories from different periods you will see that they reflect the changes which have taken place in society. What is clear though, is that love, of one kind or another, endures.

# Malachi's Cove

## Anthony Trollope

Mally Trenglos, the heroine of *Malachi's Cove*, is a surprisingly unconventional woman for Victorian times. With her bare feet, unstockinged legs and wild-flowing, black, uncombed hair, she is not at all the quiet, demure and corseted lady we are accustomed to seeing in television costume dramas.

Mally is a young woman who earns a living for herself and her grandfather collecting seaweed from a rocky cove off the Cornish coast. When Bartholomew Gunliffe, 'a fine young fellow', comes down the cliff to gather seaweed on her patch, she feels such a passion of hatred for the man and his pony that she would like to see them both dead. However, when Bartholomew's life is suddenly in danger from the stormy seas, Mally's feelings change.

*Malachi's Cove* was first published in the *Good Word* magazine in 1864. Since it would have been too shocking for a Victorian audience to have read of Mally's passionate feelings, **Anthony Trollope** (1815–1882) uses the stormy weather and turbulent sea as metaphors to describe the intensity of the experience.

*Malachi's Cove* can be described as a traditionally-shaped story. The scene is set, the place and characters are all described in detail and the emotions unfold gradually as the story develops. As you read through, it is worthwhile stopping to see if you can predict what will happen in the end.

On the northern coast of Cornwall, between Tintagel and Bossiney, down on the very margin of the sea, there lived not long since an old man who got his living by saving seaweed from the waves, and selling it for manure. The cliffs there are bold and fine, and the sea beats in upon them from the north with a grand violence. I doubt whether it be not the finest morsel of cliff scenery in England, though it is beaten by many portions of the west coast of Ireland, and perhaps also by spots in Wales and Scotland. Cliffs should be nearly precipitous, they should be broken in their outlines, and should barely admit here and there of an insecure passage from their summit to the sand at their feet. The sea should come, if not up to them, at least very near to them, and then, above all things, the water below them should be blue, and not of that dead leaden colour which is so familiar to us in England. At Tintagel all these requisites are there, except that bright blue colour which is so lovely. But the cliffs themselves are bold and well broken, and the margin of sand at high water is very narrow – so narrow that at spring-tides there is barely a footing there.

Close upon this margin was the cottage or hovel of Malachi Trenglos, the old man of whom I have spoken. But Malachi, or old Glos, as he was commonly called by the people around him, had not built his house absolutely upon the sand. There was a fissure in the rock so great that at the top it formed a narrow ravine, and so complete from the summit to the base that it afforded an opening for a steep and rugged track from the top of the rock to the bottom. This fissure was so wide at the bottom that it had afforded space for Trenglos to fix his habitation on a foundation of rock, and here he had lived for many years. It was told of him that in the early days of his trade he had always carried the weed in a basket on his back to the top, but latterly he had been possessed of a donkey, which had been trained to go up and down the steep track with a single pannier over his loins, for the rocks would not admit of panniers hanging by his side; and for this assistant he had built a shed adjoining his own, and almost as large as that in which he himself resided.

But, as years went on, old Glos procured other assistance than that of the donkey, or, as I should rather say, Providence supplied him with other help; and, indeed, had it not been so, the old man must have given up his cabin and his independence and gone into the workhouse at Camelford. For rheumatism had afflicted him, old age had bowed him till he was nearly double, and by degrees he became unable to attend the donkey on its upward passage to the world above, or even to assist in rescuing the coveted weed from the waves.

At the time to which our story refers Trenglos had not been up the cliff for twelve months, and for the last six months he had done nothing towards the furtherance of his trade, except to take the money and keep it, if any of it was kept, and occasionally to shake down a bundle of fodder for the donkey. The real work of the business was done altogether by Mahala Trenglos, his granddaughter.

Mally Trenglos was known to all the farmers around the coast, and to all the small tradespeople in Camelford. She was a wild-looking, almost unearthly creature, with wild-flowing, black, uncombed hair, small in stature, with small hands and bright black eyes; but people said that she was very strong, and the children around declared that she worked day and night and knew nothing of fatigue. As to her age there were many doubts. Some said she was ten, and others five-and-twenty, but the reader may be allowed to know that at this time she had in truth passed her twentieth birthday. The old people spoke well of Mally, because she was so good to her grandfather; and it was said of her that though she carried to him a little gin and tobacco almost daily, she bought nothing for herself; – and as to the gin, no one who looked at her would accuse her of meddling with that. But she had no friends and but few acquaintances among people of her own age. They said that she was fierce and ill-natured, that she had not a good word for any one, and that she was, complete at all points, a thorough little vixen. The young men did not care for her; for, as regarded dress, all days were alike with her. She never made herself smart on Sundays. She was generally without stockings, and seemed to care not at all to exercise any of those feminine attractions which might have been hers had she studied to attain them. All days were the same to her in regard to dress; and, indeed, till lately, all days had, I fear, been the same to her in other respects. Old Malachi had never been seen inside a place of worship since he had taken to live under the cliff.

But within the last two years Mally had submitted herself to the teaching of the clergyman at Tintagel, and had appeared at church on Sundays, if not absolutely with punctuality, at any rate so often that no one who knew the peculiarity of her residence was disposed to quarrel with her on that subject. But she made no difference in her dress on these occasions. She took her place on a low stone seat just inside the church door, clothed as usual in her thick red serge petticoat and loose brown serge jacket, such being the apparel which she had found to be best adapted for her hard and perilous work among the waters. She had pleaded to the clergyman when he attacked her on the subject of church attendance with vigour that she had got no church-going clothes. He had explained to her that she would be received there without distinction to her clothing. Mally had taken him at his word, and had gone, with a courage which certainly deserved admiration, though I doubt whether there was not mingled with it an obstinacy which was less admirable.

For people said that old Glos was rich, and that Mally might have proper clothes if she chose to buy them. Mr Polwarth, the clergyman, who, as the old man could not come to him, went down the rocks to the old man, did make some hint on the matter in Mally's absence. But old Glos, who had been patient with him on other matters, turned upon him so angrily when he made an allusion to money, that Mr Polwarth found himself obliged to give that matter up, and Mally continued to sit upon the stone bench in her short serge petticoat, with her long hair streaming down her face. She did so far sacrifice to decency as on such occasions to tie up her black hair with an old shoestring. So tied it would remain through the Monday and Tuesday, but by Wednesday afternoon Mally's hair had generally managed to escape.

As to Mally's indefatigable industry there could be no manner of doubt, for the quantity of seaweed which she and the donkey amassed between them was very surprising. Old Glos, it was declared, had never collected half what Mally gathered together; but then the article was becoming cheaper, and it was necessary that the exertion should be greater. So Mally and the donkey toiled and toiled, and the seaweed came up in heaps which surprised those who looked at her little hands and light form. Was there not someone who helped her at nights, some fairy, or demon, or the like? Mally was so snappish in her answers to people that she had no right to be surprised if ill-natured things were said of her.

No one ever heard Mally Trenglos complain of her work, but about this time she was heard to make great and loud complaints of the treatment she received from some of her neighbours. It was known that she went with her plaints to Mr Polwarth; and when he could not help her, or did not give her such instant help as she needed, she went – ah, so foolishly! to the office of a certain attorney at Camelford, who was not likely to prove himself a better friend than Mr Polwarth.

Now the nature of her injury was as follows. The place in which she collected her seaweed was a little cove; – the people had come to call it Malachi's Cove from the name of the old man who lived there; – which was so formed, that the margin of the sea therein could only be reached by the passage from the top down to Trenglos's hut. The breadth of the cove when the sea was out might perhaps be two hundred yards, and on each side the rocks ran out in such a way that both from north and south the domain of Trenglos was guarded from intruders. And this locality had been well chosen for its intended purpose.

There was a rush of the sea into the cove, which carried there large, drifting masses of seaweed, leaving them among the rocks when the tide was out. During the equinoctial* winds of the spring and autumn the supply would never fail; and even when the sea was calm, the long, soft, salt-bedewed, trailing masses of the weed, could be gathered there when they could not be found elsewhere for miles along the coast. The task of getting the weed from the breakers was often difficult and dangerous – so difficult that much of it was left to be carried away by the next incoming tide.

Mally doubtless did not gather half the crop that was there at her feet. What was taken by the returning waves she did not regret; but when interlopers came upon her cove, and gathered her wealth, – her grandfather's wealth, beneath her eyes, then her heart was broken. It was this interloping, this

---

*equinoctial: around the time of the spring and autumn equinoxes (March/September)

intrusion, that drove poor Mally to the Camelford attorney. But, alas, though the Camelford attorney took Mally's money, he could do nothing for her, and her heart was broken!

She had an idea, in which no doubt her grandfather shared, that the path to the cove was, at any rate, their property. When she was told that the cove, and sea running into the cove, were not the freeholds of her grandfather, she understood that the statement might be true. But what then as to the use of the path? Who had made the path what it was? Had she not painfully, wearily, with exceeding toil, carried up bits of rock with her own little hands, that her grandfather's donkey might have footing for his feet? Had she not scraped together crumbs of earth along the face of the cliff that she might make easier to the animal the track of that rugged way? And now, when she saw big farmer's lads coming down with other donkeys, – and, indeed, there was one who came with a pony; no boy, but a young man, old enough to know better than rob a poor old man and a young girl, – she reviled the whole human race, and swore that the Camelford attorney was a fool.

Any attempt to explain to her that there was still weed enough for her was worse than useless. Was it not all hers and his, or, at any rate, was not the sole way to it his and hers? And was not her trade stopped and impeded? Had she not been forced to back her laden donkey down, twenty yards she said, but it had, in truth, been five, because Farmer Gunliffe's son had been in the way with his thieving pony? Farmer Gunliffe had wanted to buy her weed at his own price, and because she had refused he had set on his thieving son to destroy her in this wicked way.

'I'll hamstring the beast the next time as he's down here!' said Mally to old Glos, while the angry fire literally streamed from her eyes.

Farmer Gunliffe's small homestead, – he held about fifty acres of land, was close by the village of Tintagel, and not a mile from the cliff. The sea-wrack, as they call it, was pretty well the only manure within his reach, and no doubt he thought it hard that he should be kept from using it by Mally Trenglos and her obstinacy.

'There's heaps of other coves, Barty,' said Mally to Barty Gunliffe, the farmer's son.

'But none so nigh, Mally, nor yet none that fills 'emselves as this place.'

Then he explained to her that he would not take the weed that came up close to hand. He was bigger than she was, and stronger, and would get it from the outer rocks, with which she never meddled. Then, with scorn in her eye, she swore that she could get it where he durst not venture, and repeated her threat of hamstringing the pony. Barty laughed at her wrath, jeered her because of her wild hair, and called her a mermaid.

'I'll mermaid you!' she cried. 'Mermaid, indeed! I wouldn't be a man to come and rob a poor girl and an old cripple. But you're no man, Barty Gunliffe! You're not half a man.'

Nevertheless, Bartholomew Gunliffe was a very fine young fellow as far as the eye went. He was about five feet eight inches high, with strong arms and legs, with light curly brown hair and blue eyes. His father was but in a small way as a farmer, but, nevertheless, Barty Gunliffe was well thought of among the girls around. Everybody liked Barty, – excepting only Mally Trenglos, and she hated him like poison.

Barty, when he was asked why so good-natured a lad as he persecuted a poor girl and an old man, threw himself upon the justice of the thing. It wouldn't do at all, according to his view, that any single person should take upon himself to own that which God Almighty sent as the common property of all. He would do Mally no harm, and so he had told her. But Mally was a vixen, – a wicked little vixen; and she must be taught to have a civil tongue in her head. When once Mally would speak him civil as he went for weed, he would get his father to pay the old man some sort of toll for the use of the path.

'Speak him civil?' said Mally. 'Never; not while I have a tongue in my mouth!' And I fear old Glos encouraged her rather than otherwise in her view of the matter.

But her grandfather did not encourage her to hamstring the pony. Hamstringing a pony would be a serious thing, and old Glos thought it might be very awkward for both of them if Mally were put into prison. He suggested, therefore, that all manner of impediments should be put in the way of the pony's feet, surmising that the well-trained donkey might be able to work in spite of them. And Barty Gunliffe, on his next descent, did find the passage very awkward when he came near to Malachi's hut, but he made his way down, and poor Mally saw the lumps of rock at which she had laboured so hard pushed on one side or rolled out of the way with a steady persistency of injury towards herself that almost drove her frantic.

'Well, Barty, you're a nice boy,' said old Glos, sitting in the doorway of the hut, as he watched the intruder.

'I ain't a doing no harm to none as doesn't harm me,' said Barty. 'The sea's free to all, Malachi.'

'And the sky's free to all, but I mustn't get up on the top of your big barn to look at it,' said Mally, who was standing among the rocks with a long hook in her hand. The long hook was the tool with which she worked in dragging the weed from the waves. 'But you ain't got no justice, nor yet no sperrit, or you wouldn't come here to vex an old man like he.'

'I didn't want to vex him, nor yet to vex you, Mally. You let me be for a while, and we'll be friends yet.'

'Friends!' exclaimed Mally. 'Who'd have the likes of you for a friend? What are you moving them stones for? Them stones belongs to grandfather.' And in her wrath she made a movement as though she were going to fly at him.

'Let him be, Mally,' said the old man; 'let him be. He'll get his punishment. He'll come to be drowned some day if he comes down here when the wind is in shore.'

'That he may be drowned then!' said Mally, in her anger. 'If he was in the big hole there among the rocks, and the sea running in at half-tide, I wouldn't lift a hand to help him out.'

'Yes, you would, Mally; you'd fish me up with your hook like a big stick of seaweed.'

She turned from him with scorn as he said this, and went into the hut. It was time for her to get ready for her work, and one of the great injuries done her lay in this, – that such a one as Barty Gunliffe should come and look at her during her toil among the breakers.

It was an afternoon in April, and the hour was something after four o'clock. There had been a heavy wind from the north-west all the morning, with gusts of rain, and the sea-gulls had been in and out of the cove all the day, which was a sure sign to Mally that the incoming tide would cover the rocks with weed.

The quick waves were now returning with wonderful celerity* over the low reefs, and the time had come at which the treasure must be seized, if it was to be garnered on that day. By seven o'clock it would be growing dark, at nine it would be high water, and before daylight the crop would be carried out again if not collected. All this Mally understood very well, and some of this Barty was beginning to understand also.

As Mally came down with her bare feet, bearing her long hook in her hand, she saw Barty's pony standing patiently on the sand, and in her heart she longed to attack the brute. Barty at this moment, with a common three-pronged fork in his hand, was standing down on a large rock, gazing forth towards the waters. He had declared that he would gather the weed only at places which were inaccessible to Mally, and he was looking out that he might settle where he would begin.

'Let 'un be, let 'un be,' shouted the old man to Mally, as he saw her take a step towards the beast, which she hated almost as much as she hated the man.

Hearing her grandfather's voice through the wind, she desisted from her purpose, if any purpose she had had, and went forth to her work. As she passed down the cove, and scrambled in among the rocks, she saw Barty still standing on his perch; out beyond, the white-curling waves were cresting and breaking themselves with violence, and the wind was howling among the caverns and abutments of the cliff.

Every now and then there came a squall of rain, and though there was sufficient light, the heavens were black with clouds. A scene more beautiful might hardly be found by those who love the glories of the coast. The light for such objects was perfect. Nothing could exceed the grandeur of the colours, – the blue of the open sea, the white of the breaking waves, the

---

*celerity: speed

yellow sands, or the streaks of red and brown which gave such richness to the cliffs.

But neither Mally nor Barty were thinking of such things as these. Indeed they were hardly thinking of their trade after its ordinary forms. Barty was meditating how he might best accomplish his purpose of working beyond the reach of Mally's feminine powers, and Mally was resolving that wherever Barty went she would go farther.

And, in many respects, Mally had the advantage. She knew every rock in the spot, and was sure of those which gave a good foothold, and sure also of those which did not. And then her activity had been made perfect by practice for the purpose to which it was to be devoted. Barty, no doubt, was stronger than she, and quite as active. But Barty could not jump among the waves from one stone to another as she could do, nor was he as yet able to get aid in his work from the very force of the water as she could get it. She had been hunting seaweed in that cove since she had been an urchin of six years old, and she knew every hole and corner and every spot of vantage. The waves were her friends, and she could use them. She could measure their strength, and knew when and where it would cease.

Mally was great down in the salt pools of her own cove, – great, and very fearless. As she watched Barty make his way forward from rock to rock, she told herself, gleefully, that he was going astray. The curl of the wind as it blew into the cove would not carry the weed up to the northern buttresses of the cove; and then there was the great hole just there, – the great hole of which she had spoken when she wished him evil.

And now she went to work, hooking up the dishevelled hairs of the ocean, and landing many a cargo on the extreme margin of the sand, from whence she would be able in the evening to drag it back before the invading waters would return to reclaim the spoil.

And on his side also Barty made his heap up against the northern buttresses of which I have spoken. Barty's heap became big and still bigger, so that he knew, let the pony work as he might, he could not take it all up that evening. But still it was not as large as Mally's heap. Mally's hook was better than his fork, and Mally's skill was better than his strength. And when he failed in some haul Mally would jeer him with a wild, weird laughter, and shriek to him through the wind that he was not half a man. At first he answered her with laughing words, but before long, as she boasted of her success and pointed to his failure, he became angry, and then he answered her no more. He became angry with himself, in that he missed so much of the plunder before him.

The broken sea was full of the long straggling growth which the waves had torn up from the bottom of the ocean, but the masses were carried past him, away from him, – nay, once or twice over him; and then Mally's weird voice would sound in his ear, jeering him. The gloom among the rocks was now becoming thicker and thicker, the tide was beating in with increased strength, and the gusts of wind came with quicker and greater violence. But still he worked on. While Mally worked he would work, and he would work for some time after she was driven in. He would not be beaten by a girl.

The great hole was now full of water, but of water which seemed to be boiling as though in a pot. And the pot was full of floating masses, – large treasures of seaweed which were thrown to and fro upon its surface, but lying there so thick that one would seem almost able to rest upon it without sinking.

Mally knew well how useless it was to attempt to rescue aught from the fury of that boiling cauldron. The hole went in under the rocks, and the side of it towards the shore lay high, slippery, and steep. The hole, even at low water, was never empty; and Mally believed that there was no bottom to it. Fish thrown in there could escape out to the ocean, miles away, – so Mally in her softer moods would tell the visitors to the cove. She knew the hole well. Poulnadioul she was accustomed to call it; which was supposed, when translated, to mean that this was the hole of the Evil One. Never did Mally attempt to make her own of weed which had found its way into that pot.

But Barty Gunliffe knew no better, and she watched him as he endeavoured to steady himself on the treacherously slippery edge of the pool. He fixed himself there and made a haul, with some small success. How he managed it she hardly knew, but she stood still for a while watching him anxiously, and then she saw him slip. He slipped, and recovered himself; – slipped again, and again recovered himself.

'Barty, you fool!' she screamed, 'if you get yourself pitched in there, you'll never come out no more.'

Whether she simply wished to frighten him, or whether her heart relented and she had thought of his danger with dismay, who shall say? She could not have told herself. She hated him as much as ever, – but she could hardly have wished to see him drowned before her eyes.

'You go on, and don't mind me,' said he, speaking in a hoarse, angry tone.

'Mind you! – who minds you?' retorted the girl. And then she again prepared herself for her work.

But as she went down over the rocks with her long hook balanced in her hands, she suddenly heard a splash, and, turning quickly round, saw the body of her enemy tumbling amidst the eddying waves in the pool. The tide had now come up so far that every succeeding wave washed into it and over it from the side nearest to the sea, and then ran down again back from the rocks, as the rolling wave receded, with a noise like the fall of a cataract*. And then, when the surplus water had retreated for a moment, the surface of the pool would be partly calm, though the fretting bubbles would still boil up and down, and there was even a simmer on the surface, as though, in truth, the cauldron were heated. But this time of comparative rest was but a moment, for the succeeding breaker would come up almost as soon as the foam of the preceding one had gone, and then again the waters would be dashed upon the rocks, and the sides would echo with the roar of the angry wave.

Instantly Mally hurried across to the edge of the pool, crouching down upon her hands and knees for security as she did so. As a wave receded, Barty's head and face was carried round near to her, and she could see that his forehead was covered with blood. Whether he were alive or dead she did not

*cataract: waterfall

know. She had seen nothing but his blood, and the light-coloured hair of his head lying amidst the foam. Then his body was drawn along by the suction of the retreating wave; but the mass of water that escaped was not on this occasion large enough to carry the man out with it.

Instantly Mally was at work with her hook, and getting it fixed into his coat, dragged him towards the spot on which she was kneeling. During the half minute of repose she got him so close that she could touch his shoulder. Straining herself down, laying herself over the long bending handle of the hook, she strove to grasp him with her right hand. But she could not do it; she could only touch him.

Then came the next breaker, forcing itself on with a roar, looking to Mally as though it must certainly knock her from her resting-place, and destroy them both. But she had nothing for it but to kneel, and hold by her hook.

What prayer passed through her mind at that moment for herself or for him, or for that old man who was sitting unconsciously up at the cabin, who can say? The great wave came and rushed over her as she lay almost prostrate, and when the water was gone from her eyes, and the tumult of the foam, and the violence of the roaring breaker had passed by her, she found herself at her length upon the rock, while his body had been lifted up, free from her hook, and was lying upon the slippery ledge, half in the water and half out of it. As she looked at him, in that instant, she could see that his eyes were open and that he was struggling with his hands.

'Hold by the hook, Barty,' she cried, pushing the stick of it before him, while she seized the collar of his coat in her hands.

Had he been her brother, her lover, her father she could not have clung to him with more of the energy of despair. He did contrive to hold by the stick which she had given him, and when the succeeding wave had passed by, he was still on the ledge. In the next moment she was seated a yard or two above the hole, in comparative safety, while Barty lay upon the rocks with his still bleeding head resting upon her lap.

What could she do now? She could not carry him; and in fifteen minutes the sea would be up where she was sitting. He was quite insensible, and very pale, and the blood was coming slowly, – very slowly, – from the wound on his forehead. Ever so gently she put her hand upon his hair to move it back from his face; and then she bent over his mouth to see if he breathed, and as she looked at him she knew that he was beautiful.

What would she not give that he might live? Nothing now was so precious to her as his life, – as this life which she had so far rescued from the waters. But what could she do? Her grandfather could scarcely get himself down over the rocks, if indeed he could succeed in doing so much as that. Could she drag the wounded man backwards, if it were only a few feet, so that he might lie above the reach of the waves till further assistance could be procured?

She set herself to work and she moved him, almost lifting him. As she did so she wondered at her own strength, but she was very strong at that moment. Slowly, tenderly, falling on the rocks herself so that he might fall on her, she got him back to the margin of the sand, to a spot which the waters would not reach for the next two hours.

Here her grandfather met them, having seen at last what had happened from the door.

'Dada,' she said, 'he fell into the pool yonder, and was battered against the rocks. See there at his forehead.'

'Mally, I'm thinking that he's dead already,' said old Glos, peering down over the body.

'No, dada; he is not dead; but mayhap he's dying. But I'll go at once up to the farm.'

'Mally,' said the old man, 'look at his head. They'll say we murdered him.'

'Who'll say so? Who'll lie like that? Didn't I pull him out of the hole?'

'What matters that? His father'll say we killed him.'

It was manifest to Mally that whatever one might say hereafter, her present course was plain before her. She must run up the path to Gunliffe's farm and get necessary assistance. If the world were as bad as her grandfather said, it would be so bad that she would not care to live longer in it. But be that as it might, there was no doubt as to what she must do now.

So away she went as fast as her naked feet could carry her up the cliff. When at the top she looked round to see if any person might be within ken, but she saw no one. So she ran with all her speed along the headland of the cornfield which led in the direction of old Gunliffe's house, and as she drew near to the homestead she saw that Barty's mother was leaning on the gate. As she approached she attempted to call, but her breath failed her for any purpose of loud speech, so she ran on till she was able to grasp Mrs Gunliffe by the arm.

'Where's himself?' she said, holding her hand upon her beating heart that she might husband her breath.

'Who is it you mean?' said Mrs Gunliffe, who participated in the family feud against Trenglos and his granddaughter. 'What does the girl clutch me for in that way?'

'He's dying then, that's all.'

'Who is dying? Is it old Malachi? If the old man's bad, we'll send some one down.'

'It ain't dada; it's Barty! Where's himself? where's the master?' But by this time Mrs Gunliffe was in an agony of despair, and was calling out for assistance lustily. Happily Gunliffe, the father, was at hand, and with him a man from the neighbouring village.

'Will you not send for the doctor?' said Mally. 'Oh, man, you should send for the doctor!'

Whether any orders were given for the doctor she did not know, but in a very few minutes she was hurrying across the field again towards the path to the cove, and Gunliffe with the other man and his wife were following her.

As Mally went along she recovered her voice, for their step was not so quick as hers, and that which to them was a hurried movement, allowed her to get her breath again. And as she went she tried to explain to the father what had happened, saying but little, however, of her own doings in the matter. The wife hung behind listening, exclaiming every now and again that her boy was killed, and then asking wild questions as to his being yet alive. The father, as he went, said little. He was known as a silent, sober man, well spoken of for diligence and general conduct, but supposed to be stern and very hard when angered.

As they drew near to the top of the path the other man whispered something to him, and then he turned round upon Mally and stopped her.

'If he has come by his death between you, your blood shall be taken for his,' said he.

Then the wife shrieked out that her child had been murdered, and Mally, looking round into the faces of the three, saw that her grandfather's words had come true. They suspected her of having taken the life, in saving which she had nearly lost her own.

She looked round at them with awe in her face, and then, without saying a word, preceded them down the path. What had she to answer when such a charge as that was made against her? If they chose to say that she pushed him into the pool and hit him with her hook as he lay amidst the waters, how could she show that it was not so?

Poor Mally knew little of the law of evidence, and it seemed to her that she was in their hands. But as she went down the steep track with a hurried step, – a step so quick that they could not keep up with her, – her heart was very full, – very full and very high. She had striven for the man's life as though he had been her brother. The blood was yet not dry on her own legs and arms, where she had torn them in his service. At one moment she had felt sure that she would die with him in that pool. And now they said that she had murdered him! It may be that he was not dead, and what would he say if ever he should speak again? Then she thought of that moment when his eyes had opened, and he had seemed to see her. She had no fear for herself, for her heart was very high. But it was full also, – full of scorn, disdain, and wrath.

When she had reached the bottom, she stood close to the door of the hut waiting for them, so that they might precede her to the other group, which was there in front of them, at a little distance on the sand.

'He is there, and dada is with him. Go and look at him,' said Mally.

The father and mother ran on stumbling over the stones, but Mally remained behind by the door of the hut.

Barty Gunliffe was lying on the sand where Mally had left him, and old Malachi Trenglos was standing over him, resting himself with difficulty upon a stick.

'Not a move he's moved since she left him,' said he; 'not a move. I put his head on the old rug as you see, and I tried 'un with a drop of gin, but he wouldn't take it, – he wouldn't take it.'

'Oh, my boy! my boy!' said the mother, throwing herself beside her son upon the sand.

'Haud your tongue, woman,' said the father, kneeling down slowly by the lad's head, 'whimpering that way will do 'un no good.'

Then having gazed for a minute or two upon the pale face beneath him, he looked up sternly into that of Malachi Trenglos.

The old man hardly knew how to bear this terrible inquisition.

'He would come,' said Malachi; 'he brought it all upon hisself.'

'Who was it struck him?' said the father.

'Sure he struck hisself, as he fell among the breakers.'

'Liar!' said the father, looking up at the old man.

'They have murdered him! – they have murdered him!' shrieked the mother.

'Haud your peace, woman!' said the husband again. 'They shall give us blood for blood.'

Mally, leaning against the corner of the hovel, heard it all, but did not stir. They might say what they liked. They might make it out to be murder. They might drag her and her grandfather to Camelford gaol, and then to Bodmin, and the gallows; but they could not take from her the conscious feeling that was her own. She had done her best to save him, – her very best. And she had saved him!

She remembered her threat to him before they had gone down on the rocks together, and her evil wish. Those words had been very wicked; but since that she had risked her life to save his. They might say what they pleased of her, and do what they pleased. She knew what she knew.

The the father raised his son's head and shoulders in his arms, and called on the others to assist him in carrying Barty towards the path. They raised him between them carefully and tenderly, and lifted their burden on towards the spot at which Mally was standing. She never moved, but watched them at their work; and the old man followed them, hobbling after them with his crutch.

When they had reached the end of the hut she looked upon Barty's face, and saw that it was very pale. There was no longer blood upon the forehead, but the great gash was to be seen there plainly, with its jagged cut, and the skin livid and blue round the orifice. His light brown hair was hanging back, as she had made it to hang when she had gathered it with her hand after the big wave had passed over them. Ah, how beautiful he was in Mally's eyes with that pale face, and the sad scar upon his brow! She turned her face away, that they might not see her tears; but she did not move, nor did she speak.

But now, when they had passed the end of the hut, shuffling along with their burden, she heard a sound which stirred her. She roused herself quickly from her leaning posture, and stretched forth her head as though to listen; then she moved to follow them. Yes, they had stopped at the bottom of the path, and had again laid the body on the rocks. She heard that sound again, as of a long, long sigh, and then, regardless of any of them, she ran to the wounded man's head.

'He is not dead,' she said. 'There; he is not dead.'

As she spoke Barty's eyes opened, and he looked about him.

'Barty, my boy, speak to me,' said the mother.

Barty turned his face upon his mother, smiled, and then stared about him wildly.

'How is it with thee, lad?' said his father. Then Barty turned his face again to the latter voice, and as he did so his eyes fell upon Mally.

'Mally!' he said, 'Mally!'

It could have wanted nothing further to any of those present to teach them that, according to Barty's own view of the case, Mally had not been his enemy; and, in truth, Mally herself wanted no further triumph. That word had vindicated her, and she withdrew back to the hut.

'Dada,' she said, 'Barty is not dead, and I'm thinking they won't say anything more about our hurting him.'

Old Glos shook his head. He was glad the lad hadn't met his death there; he didn't want the young man's blood, but he knew what folk would say. The poorer he was the more sure the world would be to trample on him. Mally said what she could to comfort him, being full of comfort herself.

She would have crept up to the farm if she dared, to ask how Barty was. But her courage failed her when she thought of that, so she went to work again, dragging back the weed she had saved to the spot at which on the morrow she would load the donkey. As she did this she saw Barty's pony still standing patiently under the rock; so she got a lock of fodder and threw it down before the beast.

It had become dark down in the cove, but she was still dragging back the seaweed, when she saw the glimmer of a lantern coming down the pathway. It was a most unusual sight, for lanterns were not common down in Malachi's Cove. Down came the lantern rather slowly, – much more slowly than she was in the habit of descending, and then through the gloom she saw the figure of a man standing at the bottom of the path. She went up to him, and saw that it was Mr Gunliffe, the father.

'Is that Mally?' said Gunliffe.

'Yes, it is Mally; and how is Barty, Mr Gunliffe?'

'You must come to 'un yourself, now at once,' said the farmer. 'He won't sleep a wink till he's seed you. You must not say but you'll come.'

'Sure I'll come if I'm wanted,' said Mally.

Gunliffe waited a moment, thinking that Mally might have to prepare herself, but Mally needed no preparation. She was dripping with salt water from the weed which she had been dragging, and her elfin locks were streaming wildly from her head; but, such as she was, she was ready.

'Dada's in bed,' she said, 'and I can go now if you please.'

Then Gunliffe turned round and followed her up the path, wondering at the life which this girl led so far away from all her sex. It was now dark night, and he had found her working at the very edge of the rolling waves by herself, in the darkness, while the only human being who might seem to be her protector had already gone to his bed.

When they were at the top of the cliff Gunliffe took her by her hand, and led her along. She did not comprehend this, but she made no attempt to take her hand from his. Something he said about falling on the cliffs, but it was muttered so lowly that Mally hardly understood him. But in truth the man knew that she had saved his boy's life, and that he had injured her instead of thanking her. He was now taking her to his heart, and as words were wanting to him, he was showing his love after this silent fashion. He held her by the hand as though she were a child, and Mally tripped along at his side asking him no questions.

When they were at the farm-yard gate he stopped there for a moment.

'Mally, my girl,' he said, 'he'll not be content till he sees thee, but thou must not stay long wi' him, lass. Doctor says he's weak like, and wants sleep badly.'

Mally merely nodded her head, and then they entered the house. Mally had never been within it before, and looked about with wondering eyes at the furniture of the big kitchen. Did any idea of her future destiny flash upon her then, I wonder? But she did not pause here a moment, but was led up to the bed-room above stairs, where Barty was lying on his mother's bed.

'Is it Mally herself?' said the voice of the weak youth.

'It's Mally herself,' said the mother, 'so now you can say what you please.'

'Mally,' said he, 'Mally, it's along of you that I'm alive this moment.'

'I'll not forget it on her,' said the father, with his eyes turned away from her. 'I'll never forget it on her.'

'We hadn't a one but only him,' said the mother, with her apron up to her face.

'Mally, you'll be friends with me now?' said Barty.

To have been made lady of the manor of the cove for ever, Mally couldn't have spoken a word now. It was not only that the words and presence of the people there cowed her and made her speechless, but the big bed, and the looking-glass, and the unheard-of wonders of the chamber, made her feel her own insignificance. But she crept up to Barty's side, and put her hand upon his.

'I'll come and get the weed, Mally; but it shall all be for you,' said Barty.

'Indeed, you won't then, Barty dear,' said the mother; 'you'll never go near the awesome place again. What would we do if you were took from us?'

'He mustn't go near the hole if he does,' said Mally, speaking at last in a solemn voice, and imparting the knowledge which she had kept to herself while Barty was her enemy; ''specially not if the wind's any way from the nor'rard*.'

'She'd better go down now,' said the father.

Barty kissed the hand which he held, and Mally, looking at him as he did so, thought that he was like an angel.

'You'll come and see us tomorrow, Mally?' said he.

To this she made no answer, but followed Mrs Gunliffe out of the room. When they were down in the kitchen the mother had tea for her, and thick milk, and a hot cake, – all the delicacies which the farm could afford. I don't know that Mally cared much for the eating and drinking that night, but she began to think that the Gunliffes were good people, – very good people. It was better thus, at any rate, than being accused of murder and carried off to Camelford prison.

'I'll never forget it on her – never,' the father had said.

Those words stuck to her from that moment, and seemed to sound in her ears all the night. How glad she was that Barty had come down to the cove, – oh, yes, how glad! There was no question of his dying now, and as for the blow on his forehead, what harm was that to a lad like him?

'But father shall go with you,' said Mrs Gunliffe, when Mally prepared to start for the cove by herself. Mally, however, would not hear of this. She could find her way to the cove whether it was light or dark.

'Mally, thou art my child now, and I shall think of thee so,' said the mother, as the girl went off by herself.

Mally thought of this, too, as she walked home. How could she become Mrs Gunliffe's child; ah, how?

I need not, I think, tell the tale any further. That Mally did

---

*nor'rard: northward

become Mrs Gunliffe's child, and how she became so the reader will understand; and in process of time the big kitchen and all the wonders of the farmhouse were her own. The people said that Barty Gunliffe had married a mermaid out of the sea; but when it was said in Mally's hearing I doubt whether she liked it; and when Barty himself would call her a mermaid she would frown at him, and throw about her black hair, and pretend to cuff him with her little hand.

Old Glos was brought up to the top of the cliff, and lived his few remaining days under the roof of Mr Gunliffe's house; and as for the cove and the right of seaweed, from that time forth all that has been supposed to attach itself to Gunliffe's farm, and I do not know that any of the neighbours are prepared to dispute the right.

# The Legacy
## Virginia Woolf

This is a story of love, but with a puzzle to solve. Gilbert Clandon, a busy and successful politician, is looking through his dead wife's belongings and cannot understand why everything is in such perfect order when her life has ended so suddenly and unexpectedly in a tragic road accident. All her jewellery is boxed and labelled as gifts for her friends, whilst her diaries are left as a legacy for her husband. It is only through reading his wife's most private thoughts in her diaries that he begins to understand the depth of her feelings.

For the first time he understands the loyal and enduring friendship between his wife Angela and her secretary, Sissy Miller. He also learns of the secret passion his wife experienced for another man. He traces the course of their marriage from its happy beginnings and suddenly sees, for the first time, how things began to go wrong.

Written at a time when divorce was not easy, **Virginia Woolf** (1882–1941) is exploring what it means to be trapped inside an unhappy marriage when 'duty' insists that a wife must stay with her husband until 'death us do part'. *The Legacy* was published in 1944, three years after Virginia Woolf drowned herself.

'For Sissy Miller.' Gilbert Clandon, taking up the pearl brooch that lay among a litter of rings and brooches on a little table in his wife's drawing-room, read the inscription: 'For Sissy Miller, with my love.'

It was like Angela to have remembered even Sissy Miller, her secretary. Yet how strange it was, Gilbert Clandon thought once more, that she had left everything in such order – a little gift of some sort for every one of her friends. It was as if she had foreseen her death. Yet she had been in perfect health when she left the house that morning, six weeks ago; when she stepped off the kerb in Piccadilly and the car had killed her.

He was waiting for Sissy Miller. He had asked her to come; he owed her, he felt, after all the years she had been with them, this token of consideration. Yes, he went on, as he sat there waiting, it was strange that Angela had left everything in such order. Every friend had been left some little token of her affection. Every ring, every necklace, every little Chinese box – she had a passion for little boxes – had a name on it. And each had some memory for him. This he had given her; this – the enamel dolphin with the ruby eyes – she had pounced upon one day in a back street in Venice. He could remember her little cry of delight. To him, of course, she had left nothing in particular, unless it were her diary. Fifteen little volumes, bound in green leather, stood behind him on her writing table. Ever since they were married, she had kept a diary. Some of their very few – he could not call them quarrels, say tiffs – had been about that diary. When he came in and found her writing, she always shut it or put her hand over it. 'No, no, no,' he could hear her say, 'After I'm dead – perhaps.' So she had left it him, as her legacy. It was the only thing they had not shared when she was alive. But he had always taken it for granted that she would outlive him. If only she had stopped one moment, and had thought what she was doing, she would be alive now. But she had stepped straight off the kerb, the driver of the car had said at the inquest. She had given him no chance to pull up ... Here the sound of voices in the hall interrupted him.

'Miss Miller, Sir,' said the maid.

She came in. He had never seen her alone in his life, nor, of course, in tears. She was terribly distressed, and no wonder. Angela had been much more to her than an employer. She had been a friend. To himself, he thought, as he pushed a chair for her and asked her to sit down, she was scarcely distinguishable from any other woman of her kind. There were thousands of Sissy Millers – drab little women in black carrying attaché cases. But Angela, with her genius for sympathy, had discovered all sorts of qualities in Sissy Miller. She was the soul of discretion, so silent; so trustworthy, one could tell her anything, and so on.

Miss Miller could not speak at first. She sat there dabbing her eyes with her pocket handkerchief. Then she made an effort.

'Pardon me, Mr Clandon,' she said.

He murmured. Of course he understood. It was only natural. He could guess what his wife had meant to her.

'I've been so happy here,' she said, looking round. Her eyes rested on the writing table behind him. It was here they had worked – she and Angela. For Angela had her share of the duties that fall to the lot of the wife of a prominent politician. She had been the greatest help to him in his career. He had often seen her and Sissy sitting at that table – Sissy at the typewriter, taking down letters from her dictation. No doubt Miss Miller was thinking of that, too. Now all he had to do was to give her the brooch his wife had left her. A rather incongruous gift it seemed. It might have been better to have left her a sum of money, or even the typewriter. But there it was – 'For Sissy Miller, with my love.' And, taking the brooch, he gave to her with the little speech that he had prepared. He knew, he said, that she would value it. His wife had often worn it ... And she replied, as she took it, almost as if she too had prepared a speech, that it would always be a treasured possession ... She had, he supposed, other clothes upon which a pearl brooch would not look quite so incongruous. She was wearing the little black coat and skirt that seemed the uniform of her profession. Then he remembered – she was in mourning, of course. She too had had her tragedy – a brother, to whom she was devoted, had died only a week or two before Angela. In some accident was it? He could remember only Angela telling him; Angela, with her genius for sympathy, had been terribly upset. Meanwhile Sissy Miller had risen. She was putting on her gloves. Evidently she felt that she ought not to intrude. But he could not let her go without saying something about her future. What were her plans? Was there any way in which he could help her?

She was gazing at the table, where she had sat at her typewriter, where the diary lay. And, lost in her memories of Angela, she did not at once answer his suggestion that he should help her. She seemed for a moment not to understand. So he repeated:

'What are your plans, Miss Miller?'

'My plans? Oh, that's all right, Mr Clandon,' she exclaimed. 'Please don't bother yourself about me.'

He took her to mean that she was in no need of financial assistance. It would be better, he realized, to make any suggestion of that kind in a letter. All he could do now was to say as he pressed her hand, 'Remember, Miss Miller, if there's any way in which I can help you, it will be a pleasure …' Then he opened the door. For a moment, on the threshold, as if a sudden thought had struck her, she stopped.

'Mr Clandon,' she said, looking straight at him for the first time, and for the first time he was struck by the expression, sympathetic yet searching, in her eyes. 'If at any time,' [she] was saying, 'there's anything I can do to help you, remember, I shall feel it, for your wife's sake, a pleasure …'

With that she was gone. Her words and the look that went with them were unexpected. It was almost as if she believed, or hoped, that he would have need of her. A curious, perhaps a fantastic idea occurred to him as he returned to his chair. Could it be, that during all those years when he had scarcely noticed her, she, as the novelists say, had entertained a passion for him? He caught his own reflection in the glass as he passed. He was over fifty; but he could not help admitting that he was still, as the looking-glass showed him, a very distinguished-looking man.

'Poor Sissy Miller!' he said, half laughing. How he would have liked to share that joke with his wife! He turned instinctively to her diary. 'Gilbert,' he read, opening it at random, 'looked so wonderful …' It was as if she had answered his question. Of course, she seemed to say, you're very attractive to women. Of course Sissy Miller felt that too. He read on. 'How proud I am to be his wife!' And he had always been very proud to be her husband. How often when they dined out somewhere he had looked at her across the table and said to himself, She is the loveliest woman here! He read on. That first year he had been standing for Parliament. They had toured his constituency. 'When Gilbert sat down the applause was terrific. The whole audience rose and sang: "For he's a jolly good fellow." I was quite overcome.' He remembered that, too. She had been sitting on the platform beside him. He could still see the glance she cast at him, and how she had tears in her eyes. And then? He turned the pages. They had gone to Venice. He recalled that happy holiday after the election. 'We had ices at Florians.' He smiled – she was still such a child, she loved ices. 'Gilbert gave me a most interesting account of the history of Venice. He told me that the Doges ...' she had written it all out in her schoolgirl hand. One of the delights of travelling with Angela had been that she was so eager to learn. She was so terribly ignorant, she used to say, as if that were not one of her charms. And then – he opened the next volume – they had come back to London. 'I was so anxious to make a good impression. I wore my wedding dress.' He could see her now sitting next to old Sir Edward; and making a conquest of that formidable old man, his chief. He read on rapidly, filling scene after scene from her scrappy fragments. 'Dined at the House of Commons ... To an evening party at the Lovegroves. Did I realize my responsibility, Lady L. asked me, as Gilbert's wife?' Then as the years passed – he took another volume from the writing table – he had become more and more absorbed in his work. And she, of course, was more often alone. It had been a great grief to her, apparently, that they had had no children. 'How I wish,' one entry read, 'that Gilbert had a son!' Oddly enough he had never much regretted that himself. Life had been so full, so rich as it was. That year he had been given a minor post in the government. A minor post only, but her comment was: 'I am quite certain now that he will be Prime Minister!' Well, if things had gone differently, it might have been so. He paused here to speculate upon what might have been. Politics was a gamble, he reflected; but the game wasn't over yet. Not at fifty. He cast his eyes rapidly over more pages, full of the little trifles, the insignificant, happy, daily trifles that had made up her life.

He took up another volume and opened it at random. 'What a coward I am! I let the chance slip again. But it seemed selfish to bother him about my own affairs, when he has so much to think about. And we so seldom have an evening alone.' What was the meaning of that? Oh here was the explanation – it referred to her work in the East End. 'I plucked up courage and talked to Gilbert at last. He was so kind, so good. He made no objection.' He remembered that conversation. She had told him that she felt so idle, so useless. She wished to have some work of her own.

She wanted to do something – she had blushed so prettily, he remembered, as she said it sitting in that very chair – to help others. He had bantered her a little. Hadn't she enough to do looking after him, after her home? Still if it amused her of course he had no objection. What was it? Some district? Some committee? Only she must promise not to make herself ill. So it seemed that every Wednesday she went to Whitechapel. He remembered how he hated the clothes she wore on those occasions. But she had taken it very seriously it seemed. The diary was full of references like this: 'Saw Mrs Jones ... She has ten children ... Husband lost his arm in an accident ... Did my best to find a job for Lily.' He skipped on. His own name occurred less frequently. His interest slackened. Some of the entries conveyed nothing to him. For example: 'Had a heated argument about socialism with B.M.' Who was B.M.? He could not fill in the initials; some woman, he supposed, that she had met on one of her committees. 'B.M. made a violent attack on the upper classes ... I walked back after the meeting with B.M. and tried to convince him. But he is so narrow-minded.' So B.M. was a man – no doubt one of those 'intellectuals' as they called themselves, who are so violent, as Angela said, and so narrow-minded. She had invited him to come and see her apparently. 'B.M. came to dinner. He shook hands with Minnie!' That note of exclamation gave another twist to his mental picture. B.M. it seemed wasn't used to parlourmaids; he had shaken hands with Minnie. Presumably he was one of those tame working men who air their views in ladies' drawing-rooms. Gilbert knew the type, and had no liking for this particular specimen, whoever B.M. might be. Here he was again. 'Went with B.M. to the Tower of London ... He said revolution is bound to come ... He said we live in a Fool's Paradise.' That was just the kind of thing B.M. would say – Gilbert could hear him. He could also see him quite distinctly – a stubby little man, with a rough beard, red tie, dressed as they always did in tweeds, who had never done an honest day's work in his life. Surely Angela had the sense to see through him? He read on. 'B.M. said some very disagreeable things about ...' The name was carefully scratched out. 'I told him I would not listen to any more abuse of ...' Again the name was obliterated. Could it have been his own name? Was that why Angela covered the page so quickly when he came in? The thought added to his growing dislike of B.M. He had had the impertinence to discuss him in this very room. Why had Angela never told him? It was very unlike her to conceal anything; she had been the soul of candour. He turned the pages, picking out every reference to B.M. 'B.M. told me the story of his childhood. His mother went out charring … When I think of it, I can hardly bear to go on living in such luxury … Three guineas for one hat!' If only she had discussed the matter with him, instead of puzzling her poor little head about questions that were much too difficult for her to understand! He had lent her books. Karl Marx. 'The Coming Revolution.' The initials B.M., B.M., B.M., recurred repeatedly. But why never the full name? There was an informality, an intimacy in the use of initials that was very unlike Angela. Had she called him B.M. to his face? He read on. 'B.M. came unexpectedly after dinner. Luckily, I was alone.' That was only a year ago. 'Luckily' – why luckily? – 'I was alone.' Where had he been that night? He checked the date in his engagement book. It had been the night of the Mansion House dinner. And B.M. and Angela had spent the evening alone! He tried to recall that evening. Was she waiting up for him when he came back? Had the room looked just as usual? Were there glasses on the table? Were the chairs drawn close together? He could remember nothing – nothing whatever, nothing except his own speech at the Mansion House dinner. It became more and more inexplicable to him – the whole situation: his wife receiving an unknown man alone. Perhaps the next volume would explain. Hastily he reached for the last of the diaries – the one she had left unfinished when she died. There on the very first page was that cursed fellow again. 'Dined alone with B.M. … He became very agitated. He said it was time we understood each other … I tried to make him listen. But he would not. He threatened that if I did not …' the rest of the page was scored over. She had written 'Egypt. Egypt. Egypt.' over the whole page. He could not make out a single word; but there could be only one interpretation: the scoundrel had asked her to become his mistress. Alone in his room! The blood rushed to Gilbert Clandon's face. He turned the pages rapidly. What had been her answer? Initials had ceased. It was simply 'he' now. 'He came again. I told him I could not come to any decision … I implored him to leave me.' He had forced himself upon her in this very house? But why hadn't she told him? How could she have hesitated for an instant? Then: 'I wrote him a letter.' Then pages were left blank. Then there was this: 'No answer to my letter.' Then more blank pages; and then this. 'He has done what he threatened.' After that – what came after that? He turned page after page. All were blank. But there, on the very day before her death, was this entry: 'Have I the courage to do it too?' That was the end.

Gilbert Clandon let the book slide to the floor. He could see her in front of him. She was standing on the kerb in Piccadilly. Her eyes stared; her fists were clenched. Here came the car …

He could not bear it. He must know the truth. He strode to the telephone.

'Miss Miller!' There was silence. Then he heard someone moving in the room.

'Sissy Miller speaking' – her voice at last answered him.

'Who,' he thundered, 'is B.M.?'

He could hear the cheap clock ticking on her mantelpiece; then a long drawn sigh. Then at last she said:

'He was my brother.'

He *was* her brother; her brother who had killed himself.

'Is there,' he heard Sissy Miller asking, 'anything that I can explain?'

'Nothing!' he cried. 'Nothing!'

He had received his legacy. She had told him the truth. She had stepped off the kerb to rejoin her lover. She had stepped off the kerb to escape from him.

# Twelve Hours – Narratives and Perspectives

## Adèle Geras

The first thing which strikes a reader is the very different style of this love story. It is told like a film, following twelve hours in the life of a mother and daughter from 3.30 on a school-day afternoon to 3.30 in the early hours of the following morning. As we cut between the mother and daughter, we discover not only what is happening (the 'narrative' of the title), but also their feelings and points of view (the 'perspectives'). The jerkiness in the way the story is told fits in with the emotional jolts the characters are feeling.

The story deals with the excitement of physical passion between lovers, and the effect this has on the close relationship between mother and daughter. Whereas Anthony Trollope used the 'crashing sea' to describe the intensity of his characters' experience so as not to offend his nineteenth-century readers, **Adèle Geras** is free to explain the desires of her characters in more open and direct ways.

She can explain what it is like to fall madly in love, to act irresponsibly, to have someone worried to death because you have stayed out until half past three in the morning. But she also plays with our expectations about love stories and manages to produce a few surprises. *Twelve Hours – Narratives and Perspectives* was published in 1985.

*3.30 p.m. Friday afternoon. Early July.*

She locked the front door behind her and walked to the corner of Marlowe Avenue trying very hard to look as though she were merely slipping out to the shops. You never knew who might be watching. She'd said so to Alex, and told him to wait for her round the corner.

As soon as she was in the car, as soon the door was shut, Alex's arms were round her. He was kissing her. She was breathless, laughing, trembling.

'Not here, Alex,' she said. 'Someone could see …'

'So what? I love you. I want you … I'm going to shout it out of this window …' He began to wind it down.

'Stop it, Alex. I haven't breathed a word to Beth.'

'She must have guessed. I'm practically a fixture in your house.'

'Well, she knows you're a friend, of course she does, but …' Linda hesitated, ' … she doesn't know the full extent.'

'Don't be so sure,' Alex said, and began to drive away. 'These teenagers know all about it. Every detail. Innocence is a thing of the past, I'm told.'

'But I'm her mother,' Linda said, sighing. 'You can imagine all kinds of things, but that's impossible … can you imagine *your* mother …?'

Alex wrinkled his nose.

'The mind boggles.'

'Exactly.'

When Beth was born, she lay in a perspex cot: you could look through and see her tiny hands like pink sea creatures, waving above the cellular blanket. I lay in bed and stared at her for hours. It wasn't only love washing over me, it was a kind of terror. I thought then: this is what always and forever means. Every single thing she does from now until the moment of my death will be of the utmost importance to me. And it is. The most important thing.

*4.00 p.m.*

Beth Taylor rang the front door bell. There was no answer. Wearily she lifted the school bag off her shoulder and rooted around in one of the pockets for the back door key and walked around, and let herself in. This was not an unusual occurrence. Linda worked as a secretary in a school nearby, and never knew if the Head was going to pop in at half past three and tell her to type out a riveting letter about the spread of nits among the second year Juniors. Also, she sometimes had to shop on the way home. There was a note on the kitchen table.

"Dear Beth,
There's a meeting after school today, and then Alex and I are going to a movie and dinner. Sorry about this, but it only came up at lunchtime. Help yourself out of the freezer for your supper and do phone Pam or Rosie or Jean to visit you, but no orgiastic teenage parties, please!
See you later,
Love,
Mum.'

Beth swore under her breath, screwed up the note and threw it into a corner. Then she telephoned Pam.

'Come over after you've had supper,' she said. 'I'm all on my own. My mum's out gallivanting again.'

'Right,' said Pam. 'See you about seven thirty.'

Before the divorce, she was always there. That was the main thing about her: her constant presence. There always used to be a smell about the kitchen of cooking. Cakes and ratatouille mixed in with her smell, like old roses. I know, I know, said the poor distraught child, turning her tear-stained face away from the TV cameras, a Broken Home. How sad, how awful, how will I ever grow up to be anything other than a delinquent … but it wasn't like that. It was what they call a 'civilized divorce'. Everyone is still friends … or says they are. I still see my dad … nothing's really changed, because I never saw him much anyway. He was always away/abroad/busy, and now he's all those things still, only not in this house. The divorce didn't make much difference to me, but it changed Mum. She got a job, and she got a freezer and now bloody Alex, who's practically my age. Alex is O.K. I suppose. She could have told me a bit earlier, though. Prepared me. That's the trouble with grown-ups. No consideration for anyone else. Selfish.

*5.00 p.m.*

'Last time I skived off, I was twelve,' Linda said.

'What did you tell them?'

'That I was sick … that I'd be back O.K. on Monday.'

'And do you feel guilty?'

'Guilty as hell, but not on their account.'

Alex turned to look at her, and raised an eyebrow.

She said: 'It's Beth ... how do you think she'd feel if she knew her mother'd been making love half the afternoon? It's naughty.'

'But nice. Like the cream cakes. Come here.'

Linda moved into the curve of Alex's arm and closed her eyes.

After Clive left, I thought I'd never feel anything again. Then Alex came to the school, and the very first time I saw him, I grew soft all over. For ages I just looked at him whenever I got the chance and wanted him like mad. I was like a kid, stupid and tongue-tied, rushing down certain corridors, going home down certain streets in the hope of bumping into him. I couldn't believe, still can hardly believe, that he felt what he said he felt. The first time he kissed me, behind the door of the stationery room (what a cliché!) I blushed and nearly fainted, like a young girl, weak under his hands. Now when I'm with him, it's like being drunk: it's heat and light and I have no control over myself. I'm not behaving in a grown-up fashion. He's ten years younger than I am. His skin is smooth like a small child's. When I'm with him, he's all I can think about. I've tried to be discreet at school, but I feel like a Ready Brek advertisement, glowing all over, all the time.

*7.45 p.m.*

'I think,' said Pam, 'that he's quite fanciable, from what I've seen.'

'He's all right, I suppose,' said Beth, 'if you like the doomed poet type: all floppy blond hair and long fingers.'

"I wouldn't say no.'

'I would,' said Beth. 'I think there's altogether too much sex about. I don't reckon it's good for you.'

'Rubbish. Who said so?'

'I've read all about it.' Beth held up her hand and ticked the points off, one by one. 'First off, you can get pregnant. Then, if you go on the pill, your hormones get mucked about, then you can get herpes and stuff like that, and then they say you can get cancer of the cervix from it. Seems a bit bloody hazardous to me.'

'When you're in love,' Pam said, 'you don't think about all that. You get carried away.'

'I call that,' Beth said, 'irresponsible. She's my mum. She's got no right to get carried away ... she's got me to think of, hasn't she?'

'But she isn't fifteen, is she? All those things you mentioned are only supposed to happen to people our age, not to mums. Probably grown-up propaganda to stop us having fun.'

'I don't know about fun so much ... it sounds a bit messy and revolting to me.'

'It's all different when you're in love,' Pam said firmly.

'But how on earth are you meant to know when you *are* in love?' Beth sighed.

Pam pondered this question for a moment. 'You know you're in love,' she said finally, 'when all that stuff *doesn't* seem messy and revolting any more.' She looked at her watch. 'Isn't it time for that movie on telly?'

> She's changed, there's no doubt about that. Her clothes are different. Well, before she only ever stood about the house and did housework, or dug in the garden, so jeans and a baggy old sweater were O.K. Now she has to have decent clothes for school, I understand that, but I don't just mean her clothes ... she's had her ears pierced, and wears long earrings that catch the light, and she's changed her perfume. It's not soft pink roses any more. It's a brown, smooth, thick smell, like fur. Perhaps Alex gave it to her. She wears blusher. I caught her putting on her make-up the other day ... her bra was pink and lacy and her bosom seemed to be slipping out over the top. Her knickers were like tiny little lace-trimmed shorts ... I asked her about them and she said they were new and did I like them, but she was blushing like crazy, all the way down her neck, and she dressed very quickly after that ... that was when I began to suspect about Alex. There's a

couple writhing around on telly this very minute. If I think of Alex and Mum doing that, I feel quite ill. I wonder if Pam really likes this film ... I wouldn't mind turning over to another channel.

*2.30 a.m.*

Linda leapt out of bed.

'Alex! Alex, wake up, for heaven's sake! Look at the time ... it'll be morning at this rate before I get home. Come on, Alex, please, wake up! Beth'll be worried frantic ... please.'

Alex yawned and stretched and smiled.

'Relax. It's O.K. I'm awake now. I'll be ready in two shakes of a lamb's tail. And don't worry about Beth. She's a big girl. She'll have gone to sleep hours ago.'

'Please hurry, Alex.' Linda sighed. 'I knew we shouldn't have come back here for coffee after dinner. I knew at the time it was a mistake.'

'No, you didn't. You couldn't wait, go on, admit it ... '

'I admit it, I admit it, now for the last time, will you get your bloody shoes on, and let's get out of here!'

I wish he could drive faster. I wish we could be home sooner. Oh, please, let Beth be O.K. Let her not be worried. Let the house not have burned to the ground, let there not be a mad axeman on the loose. Please, please, don't let me be punished. I know I shouldn't have gone back for coffee, but please let it be all right and I'll never do it again. It's just that every second since she was born I've thought about every one of my actions in relation to her. Will Beth be O.K.? Want to go to the hairdresser? Then fix someone to pick her up from school. Want to go to the movies? Find a babysitter. Beth twenty minutes late back from school? All kinds of horrors flying behind the eyes. Now that she's a little older, nearly a grown-up, I feel as though I'm able to do certain things without looking over my shoulder to make sure she's all right. But not everything. Please, Beth, be all right. Don't be angry. Please understand.

*3.30 a.m.*

'Mum, is that you?'

'Ssh. Yes it's me. Are you O.K.?' Whispering.

'You don't need to whisper. I'm not asleep.'

Linda came into Beth's room and sat on the bed. 'Haven't you been asleep at all?'

'Oh, yes, on and off. In between worrying myself sick about you ... where the hell have you been? It's bloody half past three in the morning.'

'Oh, Bethy, my love, I'm so sorry. I was having such a good time ... I just forgot about the time ... I'm really sorry. I won't do it again, I promise.'

'I thought you might have had a car crash ... you could have rung up, couldn't you, when you knew you'd be late. Couldn't you? And what are you giggling about?'

Linda had started to laugh, and now, weak from lack of sleep and relief that Beth was there, just the same under her flower-printed sheets, her laughter grew and grew until the tears were streaming down her cheeks.

'You should hear yourself ... you sound like a mother, you do honestly, and me ... I feel like a juvenile delinquent.'

'Delinquent ... yes. Juvenile ... I'm not quite so sure ...' Beth, happy to have her mother home again, even wearing new perfume, began to laugh as well.

> It's like one of those books where someone wakes up one day and she's turned into someone else. Or when a family discovers their child is really a mouse or something. There's a famous one where a guy wakes up and finds he's become this huge cockroach-type creature ... you can see someone's point of view much better from another perspective. I always used to get dead irritated when I'd come home late and see Mum peering down the road, all white-faced and frowny, but I know how she feels now. She wasn't at the movies till 3.30. She must be sleeping with Alex. That'll take some getting used to. I must get used to it. I will.

# Love: Activities

## 1 Comparing stories for wide reading

Compare and contrast the ways in which the development and expression of love is shown in:
*Malachi's Cove* by Anthony Trollope and
**either**
*The Legacy* by Virginia Woolf
**or**
*Twelve Hours – Narratives and Perspectives*
by Adèle Geras.

You might like to comment on:

- How the characters are described.
- The way changing emotions are hinted at.
- How barriers between lovers are built up or broken down.
- How love grows and finds its expression.
- The differing ways the authors describe the experience of love.
- The powerlessness of onlookers to intervene.
- How the endings make some sort of resolution.
- How the period of time in which the story was written influences what happens and the way it is told.

## 2 Opportunities for original writing

After reflecting on what you have learned from studying the stories in this section write about:

- A story where intense feelings of anger and mistrust turn to love.
- A tale of love with a puzzle to unravel.
- A collection of letters or diary extracts which reveal a growing love.
- A story with alternative viewpoints:
  - – mother and daughter
  - – father and son
  - – two lovers.
- Stormy feelings – stormy weather. Write about an encounter between two people where the changes in the weather reflect and highlight the changes in their feelings for each other.

Section 4

# Science Fiction

Science fiction has its roots in the story of *Frankenstein* written by Mary Shelley in 1818. In 1864, the French writer Jules Verne wrote *Journey to the Centre of the Earth*, and followed it a year later by writing a novel about travelling from the Earth to the Moon by space rocket. In the same year there were at least four other novels published in France about interplanetary travel. In 1895 H.G. Wells wrote *The Time Machine*, and later went on to write about an invasion by Martians in *The War of the Worlds* (1898), and in 1901 about *The First Men in the Moon*.

For a long time, writers have been attempting to predict the future. They have been interested in the possible effects of new technology on people's lives, and how people adapt to these changes. Writers have used their imaginations to think about the potential of science and also the possible dangers, and they have worked through these ideas in their stories. The stories are usually written in the third person. They often include reports and technological descriptions, with new names for the people, places and objects that the writer has invented.

The best science fiction helps us think freshly about our own world and society. Science fiction stories often take a current trend or new development and show what could happen if it is allowed to get out of hand. Some science fiction is concerned with aliens, space ships, amazing technology and other worlds. Other science fiction focuses more on the organization of society or home life in the future. Either type of science fiction will show the reader something about the concerns and values of the writer and the society he or she lives in.

# Extract from 'The Time Machine'

## H.G. Wells

**Herbert George Wells** (1866–1946) had a very important influence on the development of science fiction in Britain. *The Time Machine* was published as a short book in 1895, but in the year before that it had aroused a great deal of interest when it had appeared in instalments as a serial. The whole story is too long to include here, but the extract will give you the flavour of the whole story (which is easily available at a library or on the Internet).

Wells called his novels 'social fables' and they certainly all carry strong social messages. Wells was a committed socialist and keen to comment on the political and social issues of his day. *The Time Machine* is written as a series of after-dinner conversations in a middle-class gentleman's home, and H.G.Wells takes every opportunity to debate ideas and engage in philosophical discussions. The dinner guests include an editor, a doctor and a psychologist, but they are included to represent points of view connected with their work rather than as individual characters. They are in conversation with the Time Traveller, who has just built and travelled in his own Time Machine.

*The Time Machine* is an early example of science fiction, and not entirely typical of the genre as we would know it today. However, certain important features of the genre are easily recognizable: the interest in science and the technology of the Time Machine; the portrayal of alien life forms from the year 802,000; the environment in the future. Also typical is the social question which underpins the story. Wells is interested in exploring the future of the human race – read on to find out his vision of what we may become!

*A group of dinner guests are waiting for a scientist to join them. The scientist told them at their last meeting that he had invented a Time Machine. The dinner guests call him the Time Traveller, but they do not really believe that the Time Machine exists. The Psychologist is telling a story when the Time Traveller arrives.*

The Psychologist was in the midst of his exposition when the door from the corridor opened slowly and without noise. I was facing the door, and saw it first. 'Hallo!' I said. 'At last!' And the door opened wider, and the Time Traveller stood before us. I gave a cry of surprise. 'Good heavens! man, what's the matter?' cried the Medical Man, who saw him next. And the whole tableful turned towards the door.

He was in an amazing plight. His coat was dusty and dirty, and smeared with green down the sleeves; his hair disordered, and as it seemed to me greyer – either with dust and dirt or because its colour had actually faded. His face was ghastly pale; his chin had a brown cut on it – a cut half healed; his expression was haggard and drawn, as by intense suffering. For a moment he hesitated in the doorway, as if he had been dazzled by the light. Then he came into the room. He walked with just such a limp as I have seen in footsore tramps. We stared at him in silence, expecting him to speak.

He said not a word, but came painfully to the table, and made a motion towards the wine. The Editor filled a glass of champagne, and pushed it towards him. He drained it, and it seemed to do him good: for he looked round the table, and the ghost of his old smile flickered across his face. 'What on earth have you been up to, man?' said the Doctor. The Time Traveller did not seem to hear. 'Don't let me disturb you,' he said, with a certain faltering articulation. 'I'm all right.' He stopped, held out his glass for more, and took it off at a draught. 'That's good,' he said. His eyes grew brighter, and a faint colour came into his cheeks. His glance flickered over our faces with a certain dull approval, and then went round the warm and comfortable room. Then he spoke again, still as it were feeling his way among his words. 'I'm going to wash and dress, and then I'll come down and explain things. … Save me some of that mutton. I'm starving for a bit of meat.'

He looked across at the Editor, who was a rare visitor, and hoped he was all right. The Editor began a question. 'Tell you presently,' said the Time Traveller. 'I'm – funny! Be all right in a minute.'

He put down his glass, and walked towards the staircase door. Again I remarked his lameness and the soft padding sound of his footfall, and standing up in my place, I saw his feet as he went out. He had nothing on them but a pair of tattered blood-stained socks. Then the door closed upon him. I had half a mind to follow, till I remembered how he detested any fuss about himself. For a minute, perhaps, my mind was wool-gathering. Then, 'Remarkable Behaviour of an Eminent Scientist,' I heard the Editor say, thinking (after his wont*) in headlines. And this brought my attention back to the bright dinner-table.

'What's the game?' said the Journalist. 'Has he been doing the Amateur Cadger? I don't follow.' I met the eye of the Psychologist, and read my own interpretation in his face. I thought of the Time Traveller limping painfully upstairs. I don't think any one else had noticed his lameness.

The first to recover completely from this surprise was the Medical Man, who rang the bell – the Time Traveller hated to have servants waiting at dinner – for a hot plate. At that the Editor turned to his knife and fork with a grunt, and the Silent Man followed suit. The dinner was resumed. Conversation was exclamatory for a little while, with gaps of wonderment; and then the Editor got fervent in his curiosity. 'Does our friend eke out his modest income with a crossing? or has he his Nebuchadnezzar* phases?' he inquired. 'I feel assured it's this business of the Time Machine,' I said, and took up the Psychologist's account of our previous meeting. The new guests were frankly incredulous. The Editor raised objections. 'What WAS this time travelling? A man couldn't cover himself with dust by rolling in a paradox, could he?' And then, as the idea came home to him, he resorted to caricature. Hadn't they any clothes-brushes in the Future? The

---

*wont: custom, habit

*Nebuchadnezzar: Babylonian king who supposedly went on all fours like an animal and ate grass

Journalist too, would not believe at any price, and joined the Editor in the easy work of heaping ridicule on the whole thing. They were both the new kind of journalist – very joyous, irreverent young men. 'Our Special Correspondent in the Day after To-morrow reports,' the Journalist was saying – or rather shouting – when the Time Traveller came back. He was dressed in ordinary evening clothes, and nothing save his haggard look remained of the change that had startled me.

'I say,' said the Editor hilariously, 'these chaps here say you have been travelling into the middle of next week! Tell us all about little Rosebery, will you? What will you take for the lot?'

The Time Traveller came to the place reserved for him without a word. He smiled quietly, in his old way. 'Where's my mutton?' he said. 'What a treat it is to stick a fork into meat again!'

'Story!' cried the Editor.

'Story be damned!' said the Time Traveller. 'I want something to eat. I won't say a word until I get some peptone* into my arteries. Thanks. And the salt.'

'One word,' said I. 'Have you been time travelling?'

'Yes,' said the Time Traveller, with his mouth full, nodding his head.

'I'd give a shilling a line for a verbatim note,' said the Editor. The Time Traveller pushed his glass towards the Silent Man and rang it with his fingernail; at which the Silent Man, who had been staring at his face, started convulsively, and poured him wine. The rest of the dinner was uncomfortable. For my own part, sudden questions kept on rising to my lips, and I dare say it was the same with the others. The Journalist tried to relieve the tension by telling anecdotes of Hettie Potter. The Time Traveller devoted his attention to his dinner, and displayed the appetite of a tramp. The Medical Man smoked a cigarette, and watched the Time Traveller through his eyelashes. The Silent Man seemed even more clumsy than usual, and drank champagne with regularity and determination out of sheer nervousness. At last the Time Traveller pushed his plate away, and looked round us. 'I suppose I must apologize,' he said.

---

*peptone: product of the action of digestive enzymes on meat

'I was simply starving. I've had a most amazing time.' He reached out his hand for a cigar, and cut the end. 'But come into the smoking-room. It's too long a story to tell over greasy plates.' And ringing the bell in passing, he led the way into the adjoining room.

'You have told Blank, and Dash, and Chose about the machine?' he said to me, leaning back in his easy-chair and naming the three new guests.

'But the thing's a mere paradox,' said the Editor.

'I can't argue to-night. I don't mind telling you the story, but I can't argue. I will,' he went on, 'tell you the story of what has happened to me, if you like, but you must refrain from interruptions. I want to tell it. Badly. Most of it will sound like lying. So be it! It's true – every word of it, all the same. I was in my laboratory at four o'clock, and since then … I've lived eight days … such days as no human being ever lived before! I'm nearly worn out, but I shan't sleep till I've told this thing over to you. Then I shall go to bed. But no interruptions! Is it agreed?'

'Agreed,' said the Editor, and the rest of us echoed 'Agreed.' And with that the Time Traveller began his story as I have set it forth. He sat back in his chair at first, and spoke like a weary man. Afterwards he got more animated. In writing it down I feel with only too much keenness the inadequacy of pen and ink – and, above all, my own inadequacy – to express its quality. You read, I will suppose, attentively enough; but you cannot see the speaker's white, sincere face in the bright circle of the little lamp, nor hear the intonation of his voice. You cannot know how his expression followed the turns of his story! Most of us hearers were in shadow, for the candles in the smoking-room had not been lighted, and only the face of the Journalist and the legs of the Silent Man from the knees downward were illuminated. At first we glanced now and again at each other. After a time we ceased to do that, and looked only at the Time Traveller's face.

'I told some of you last Thursday of the principles of the Time Machine, and showed you the actual thing itself, incomplete in the workshop. There it is now, a little travel-worn, truly; and one of the ivory bars is cracked, and a brass rail bent; but the rest of it's sound enough. I expected to finish it on Friday, but on Friday, when the putting together was nearly done, I found that one of the nickel bars was exactly one inch too short, and this I had to get remade; so that the thing was not complete until this morning. It was at ten o'clock today that the first of all Time Machines began its career. I gave it a last tap, tried all the screws again, put one more drop of oil on the quartz rod, and sat myself in the saddle. I suppose a suicide who holds a pistol to his skull feels much the same wonder at what will come next as I felt then. I took the starting lever in one hand and the stopping one in the other, pressed the first, and almost immediately the second. I seemed to reel; I felt a nightmare sensation of falling; and, looking round, I saw the laboratory exactly as before. Had anything happened? For a moment I suspected that my intellect had tricked me. Then I noted the clock. A moment before, as it seemed, it had stood at a minute or so past ten; now it was nearly half-past three!

'I drew a breath, set my teeth, gripped the starting lever with both hands, and went off with a thud. The laboratory got hazy and went dark. Mrs Watchett came in and walked, apparently without seeing me, towards the garden door. I suppose it took her a minute or so to traverse the place, but to me she seemed to shoot across the room like a rocket. I pressed the lever over to its extreme position. The night came like the turning out of a lamp, and in another moment came to-morrow. The laboratory grew faint and hazy, then fainter and ever fainter. To-morrow night came black, then day again, night again, day again, faster and faster still. An eddying murmur filled my ears, and a strange, dumb confusedness descended on my mind.

'I am afraid I cannot convey the peculiar sensations of time travelling. They are excessively unpleasant. There is a feeling exactly like that one has upon a switchback – of a helpless headlong motion! I felt the same horrible anticipation, too, of an imminent smash. As I put on pace, night followed day like the flapping of a black wing. The dim suggestion of the laboratory seemed presently to fall away from me, and I saw the sun hopping swiftly across the sky, leaping it every minute, and every minute marking a day. I supposed the laboratory had been destroyed and I had come into the open air. I had a dim impression of scaffolding, but I was already going too fast to be conscious of any moving things. The slowest snail that ever crawled dashed by too fast for me. The twinkling succession of darkness and light was excessively painful to the eye. Then, in the intermittent darknesses, I saw the moon spinning swiftly through her quarters from new to full, and had a faint glimpse of the circling stars. Presently, as I went on, still gaining velocity, the palpitation of night and day merged into one continuous greyness; the sky took on a wonderful deepness of blue, a splendid luminous colour like that of early twilight; the jerking sun became a streak of fire, a brilliant arch, in space; the moon a fainter fluctuating band; and I could see nothing of the stars, save now and then a brighter circle flickering in the blue.

'The landscape was misty and vague. I was still on the hill-side upon which this house now stands, and the shoulder rose above me grey and dim. I saw trees growing and changing like puffs of vapour, now brown, now green; they grew, spread, shivered, and passed away. I saw huge buildings rise up faint and fair, and pass like dreams. The whole surface of the earth seemed changed – melting and flowing under my eyes. The little hands upon the dials that registered my speed raced round faster and faster. Presently I noted that the sun belt swayed up and down, from solstice* to solstice, in a minute or less, and that consequently my pace was over a year a minute; and minute by minute the white snow flashed across the world, and vanished, and was followed by the bright, brief green of spring.

'The unpleasant sensations of the start were less poignant now. They merged at last into a kind of hysterical exhilaration. I remarked indeed a clumsy swaying of the machine, for which I was unable to account. But my mind was too confused to attend to it, so with a kind of madness growing upon me, I flung myself into futurity. At first I scarce thought of stopping, scarce thought of anything but these new sensations. But presently a fresh series of impressions grew up in my mind – a certain curiosity and therewith a certain dread – until at last they took complete

---

*solstice: time when the sun is at maximum distance from the equator (June/December)

possession of me. What strange developments of humanity, what wonderful advances upon our rudimentary civilization, I thought, might not appear when I came to look nearly into the dim elusive world that raced and fluctuated before my eyes! I saw great and splendid architecture rising about me, more massive than any buildings of our own time, and yet, as it seemed, built of glimmer and mist. I saw a richer green flow up the hill-side, and remain there, without any wintry intermission. Even through the veil of my confusion the earth seemed very fair. And so my mind came round to the business of stopping.

'The peculiar risk lay in the possibility of my finding some substance in the space which I, or the machine, occupied. So long as I travelled at a high velocity through time, this scarcely mattered; I was, so to speak, attenuated – was slipping like a vapour through the interstices* of intervening substances! But to come to a stop involved the jamming of myself, molecule by molecule, into whatever lay in my way; meant bringing my atoms into such intimate contact with those of the obstacle that a profound chemical reaction – possibly a far-reaching explosion – would result, and blow myself and my apparatus out of all possible dimensions – into the Unknown. This possibility had occurred to me again and again while I was making the machine; but then I had cheerfully accepted it as an unavoidable risk – one of the risks a man has got to take! Now the risk was inevitable, I no longer saw it in the same cheerful light. The fact is that insensibly, the absolute strangeness of everything, the sickly jarring and swaying of the machine, above all, the feeling of prolonged falling, had absolutely upset my nerve. I told myself that I could never stop, and with a gust of petulance I resolved to stop forthwith. Like an impatient fool, I lugged over the lever, and incontinently* the thing went reeling over, and I was flung headlong through the air.

'There was the sound of a clap of thunder in my ears. I may have been stunned for a moment. A pitiless hail was hissing round me, and I was sitting on soft turf in front of the overset machine.

---

*interstices: small spaces between things
*incontinently: immediately

Everything still seemed grey, but presently I remarked that the confusion in my ears was gone. I looked round me. I was on what seemed to be a little lawn in a garden, surrounded by rhododendron bushes, and I noticed that their mauve and purple blossoms were dropping in a shower under the beating of the hail-stones. The rebounding, dancing hail hung in a cloud over the machine, and drove along the ground like smoke. In a moment I was wet to the skin. 'Fine hospitality,' said I, 'to a man who has travelled innumerable years to see you.'

'Presently I thought what a fool I was to get wet. I stood up and looked round me. A colossal figure, carved apparently in some white stone, loomed indistinctly beyond the rhododendrons through the hazy downpour. But all else of the world was invisible.

'My sensations would be hard to describe. As the columns of hail grew thinner, I saw the white figure more distinctly. It was very large, for a silver birch-tree touched its shoulder. It was of white marble, in shape something like a winged sphinx, but the wings, instead of being carried vertically at the sides, were spread so that it seemed to hover. The pedestal, it appeared to me, was of bronze, and was thick with verdigris*. It chanced that the face was towards me; the sightless eyes seemed to watch me; there was the faint shadow of a smile on the lips. It was greatly weather-worn, and that imparted an unpleasant suggestion of disease. I stood looking at it for a little space – half a minute, perhaps, or half an hour. It seemed to advance and to recede as the hail drove before it denser or thinner. At last I tore my eyes from it for a moment and saw that the hail curtain had worn threadbare, and that the sky was lightening with the promise of the Sun.

'I looked up again at the crouching white shape, and the full temerity of my voyage came suddenly upon me. What might appear when that hazy curtain was altogether withdrawn? What might not have happened to men? What if cruelty had grown into a common passion? What if in this interval the race had lost its manliness and had developed into something inhuman, unsympathetic, and overwhelmingly powerful? I might seem some old-world savage animal, only the more dreadful and

*verdigris: green coating on copper and its alloys

disgusting for our common likeness – a foul creature to be incontinently slain.

'Already I saw other vast shapes – huge buildings with intricate parapets and tall columns, with a wooded hill-side dimly creeping in upon me through the lessening storm. I was seized with a panic fear. I turned frantically to the Time Machine, and strove hard to readjust it. As I did so the shafts of the sun smote through the thunderstorm. The grey downpour was swept aside and vanished like the trailing garments of a ghost. Above me, in the intense blue of the summer sky, some faint brown shreds of cloud whirled into nothingness. The great buildings about me stood out clear and distinct, shining with the wet of the thunderstorm, and picked out in white by the unmelted hailstones piled along their courses. I felt naked in a strange world. I felt as perhaps a bird may feel in the clear air, knowing the hawk wings above and will swoop. My fear grew to frenzy. I took a breathing space, set my teeth, and again grappled fiercely, wrist and knee, with the machine. It gave under my desperate onset and turned over. It struck my chin violently. One hand on the saddle, the other on the lever, I stood panting heavily in attitude to mount again.

'But with this recovery of a prompt retreat my courage recovered. I looked more curiously and less fearfully at this world of the remote future. In a circular opening, high up in the wall of the nearer house, I saw a group of figures clad in rich soft robes. They had seen me, and their faces were directed towards me.

'Then I heard voices approaching me. Coming through the bushes by the White Sphinx were the heads and shoulders of men running. One of these emerged in a pathway leading straight to the little lawn upon which I stood with my machine. He was a slight creature – perhaps four feet high – clad in a purple tunic, girdled at the waist with a leather belt. Sandals or buskins* – I could not clearly distinguish which – were on his feet; his legs were bare to the knees, and his head was bare. Noticing that, I noticed for the first time how warm the air was.

---

*buskins: type of sandal with long laces tied around the legs up to the knee

'He struck me as being a very beautiful and graceful creature, but indescribably frail. His flushed face reminded me of the more beautiful kind of consumptive – that hectic beauty of which we used to hear so much. At the sight of him I suddenly regained confidence. I took my hands from the machine.

'In another moment we were standing face to face, I and this fragile thing out of futurity. He came straight up to me and laughed into my eyes. The absence from his bearing of any sign of fear struck me at once. Then he turned to the two others who were following him and spoke to them in a strange and very sweet and liquid tongue.

'There were others coming, and presently a little group of perhaps eight or ten of these exquisite creatures were about me. One of them addressed me. It came into my head, oddly enough, that my voice was too harsh and deep for them. So I shook my head, and, pointing to my ears, shook it again. He came a step forward, hesitated, and then touched my hand. Then I felt other soft little tentacles upon my back and shoulders. They wanted to make sure I was real. There was nothing in this at all alarming. Indeed, there was something in these pretty little people that inspired confidence – a graceful gentleness, a certain childlike ease. And besides, they looked so frail that I could fancy myself flinging the whole dozen of them about like nine-pins. But I made a sudden motion to warn them when I saw their little pink hands feeling at the Time Machine. Happily then, when it was not too late, I thought of a danger I had hitherto forgotten, and reaching over the bars of the machine I unscrewed the little levers that would set it in motion, and put these in my pocket. Then I turned again to see what I could do in the way of communication.

'And then, looking more nearly into their features, I saw some further peculiarities in their Dresden-china type of prettiness. Their hair, which was uniformly curly, came to a sharp end at the neck and cheek; there was not the faintest suggestion of it on the face, and their ears were singularly minute. The mouths were small, with bright red, rather thin lips, and the little chins ran to a point. The eyes were large and mild; and – this may seem egotism on my part – I fancied even that there was a certain lack of the interest I might have expected in them.

'As they made no effort to communicate with me, but simply stood round me smiling and speaking in soft cooing notes to each other, I began the conversation. I pointed to the Time Machine and to myself. Then hesitating for a moment how to express time, I pointed to the sun. At once a quaintly pretty little figure in chequered purple and white followed my gesture, and then astonished me by imitating the sound of thunder.

'For a moment I was staggered, though the import of his gesture was plain enough. The question had come into my mind abruptly: were these creatures fools? You may hardly understand how it took me. You see I had always anticipated that the people of the year Eight Hundred and Two Thousand odd would be incredibly in front of us in knowledge, art, everything. Then one of them suddenly asked me a question that showed him to be on the intellectual level of one of our five-year-old children – asked me, in fact, if I had come from the sun in a thunderstorm! It let loose the judgement I had suspended upon their clothes, their frail light limbs, and fragile features. A flow of disappointment rushed across my mind. For a moment I felt that I had built the Time Machine in vain.

# The Veldt
## Ray Bradbury

*The Veldt* (which refers to areas of open grassland in South Africa) takes the reader into the future. Technology has advanced to the point where you can switch on a whole house to do the household chores and to provide entertainment. But how does this affect the families who live in those houses? Does the technology help children grow up as psychologically healthy individuals? What are the parents' responsibilities?

These are some of the questions that are explored in Ray Bradbury's story, which comes from his classic science fiction collection *The Illustrated Man*, first published in 1952. In the Prologue and Epilogue to the book, Bradbury tells the story of a traveller who meets a man who has been tattooed all over his body. These are magical tattoos – 'illustrations' – which move and act out stories of the future on the man's body. *The Veldt* is one of those stories, which the traveller finds himself almost compelled to watch. Seventeen other varied and powerful stories follow, before the sting in the tail which emerges in the Epilogue.

**Ray Bradbury** was born in America in 1920. He became a full-time writer in 1943 and is regarded as a leading exponent of the science fiction genre.

'George, I wish you'd look at the nursery.'

'What's wrong with it?'

'I don't know.'

'Well, then.'

'I just want you to look at it, is all, or call a psychologist in to look at it.'

'What would a psychologist want with a nursery?'

'You know very well what he'd want.' His wife paused in the middle of the kitchen and watched the stove busy humming to itself, making supper for four.

'It's just that the nursery is different now than it was.'

'All right, let's have a look.'

They walked down the hall of their soundproofed, Happy-life Home, which had cost them thirty thousand dollars installed, this house which clothed and fed and rocked them to sleep and played and sang and was good to them. Their approach sensitized a switch somewhere and the nursery light flicked on when they came within ten feet of it. Similarly, behind them, in the halls, lights went on and off as they left them behind, with a soft automaticity.

'Well,' said George Hadley.

They stood on the thatched floor of the nursery. It was forty feet across by forty feet long and thirty feet high; it had cost half again as much as the rest of the house. 'But nothing's too good for our children,' George had said.

The nursery was silent. It was empty as a jungle glade at hot high noon. The walls were blank and two dimensional. Now, as George and Lydia Hadley stood in the centre of the room, the walls began to purr and recede into crystalline distance, it seemed, and presently an African veldt appeared, in three dimensions; on all sides, in colours reproduced to the final pebble and bit of straw. The ceiling above them became a deep sky with a hot yellow sun.

George Hadley felt the perspiration start on his brow.

'Let's get out of the sun,' he said. 'This is a little too real. But I don't see anything wrong.'

'Wait a moment, you'll see,' said his wife.

Now the hidden odorophonics were beginning to blow a wind of odour at the two people in the middle of the baked veldtland. The hot straw smell of lion grass, the cool green smell of the hidden water hole, the great rusty smell of animals, the smell of dust like a red paprika in the hot air. And now the sounds: the thump of distant antelope feet on grassy sod, the papery rustling of vultures. A shadow passed through the sky. The shadow flickered on George Hadley's upturned, sweating face.

'Filthy creatures,' he heard his wife say.

'The vultures.'

'You see, there are the lions, far over, that way. Now they're on their way to the water hole. They've just been eating,' said Lydia. 'I don't know what.'

'Some animal.' George Hadley put his hand up to shield off the burning light from his squinted eyes. 'A zebra or a baby giraffe, maybe.'

'Are you sure?' His wife sounded peculiarly tense.

'No, it's a little late to be *sure*,' he said, amused. 'Nothing over there I can see but cleaned bone, and the vultures dropping for what's left.'

'Did you hear that scream?' she asked.

'No.'

'About a minute ago?'

'Sorry, no.'

The lions were coming. And again George Hadley was filled with admiration for the mechanical genius who had conceived this room. A miracle of efficiency selling for an absurdly low price. Every home should have one. Oh, occasionally they frightened you with their clinical accuracy, they startled you, gave you a twinge, but most of the time what fun for everyone, not only your own son and daughter, but for yourself when you felt like a quick jaunt to a foreign land, a quick change of scenery. Well, here it was!

And here were the lions now, fifteen feet away, so real, so feverishly and startlingly real that you could feel the prickling fur on your hand, and your mouth was stuffed with the dusty upholstery smell of their heated pelts, and the yellow of them was in your eyes like the yellow of an exquisite French tapestry, the yellows of lions and summer grass, and the sound of the matted lion lungs exhaling on the silent noontide, and the smell of meat from the panting, dripping mouths.

The lions stood looking at George and Lydia Hadley with terrible green-yellow eyes.

'Watch out!' screamed Lydia.

The lions came running at them.

Lydia bolted and ran. Instinctively, George sprang after her. Outside, in the hall, with the door slammed, he was laughing and she was crying, and they both stood appalled at the other's reaction.

'George!'

'Lydia! Oh, my dear poor sweet Lydia!'

'They almost got us!'

'Walls, Lydia, remember; crystal walls, that's all they are. Oh, they look real, I must admit – Africa in your parlour – but it's all dimensional superractionary, supersensitive colour film and mental tape film behind glass screens. It's all odorophonics and sonics, Lydia. Here's my handkerchief.'

'I'm afraid.' She came to him and put her body against him and cried steadily. 'Did you see? Did you *feel*? It's too real.'

'Now, Lydia … '

'You've got to tell Wendy and Peter not to read any more on Africa.'

'Of course – of course.' He patted her.

'Promise?'

'Sure.'

'And lock the nursery for a few days until I get my nerves settled.'

'You know how difficult Peter is about that. When I punished him a month ago by locking the nursery for even a few hours – the tantrum he threw! And Wendy too. They live for the nursery.'

'It's got to be locked, that's all there is to it.'

'All right.' Reluctantly he locked the huge door. 'You've been working too hard. You need a rest.'

'I don't know – I don't know,' she said, blowing her nose, sitting down in a chair that immediately began to rock and comfort her. 'Maybe I don't have enough to do. Maybe I have time to think too much. Why don't we shut the whole house off for a few days and take a vacation?'

'You mean you want to fry my eggs for me?'

'Yes.' She nodded.

'And darn my socks?'

'Yes.' A frantic, watery-eyed nodding.

'And sweep the house?'

'Yes, yes – oh, yes!'

'But I thought that's why we bought this house, so we wouldn't have to do anything?'

'That's just it. I feel like I don't belong here. The house is wife and mother now and nursemaid. Can I compete with an African veldt? Can I give a bath and scrub the children as efficiently or quickly as the automatic scrub bath can? I can not. And it isn't just me. It's you. You've been awfully nervous lately.'

'I suppose I have been smoking too much.'

'You look as if you didn't know what to do with yourself in this house, either. You smoke a little more every morning and drink a little more every afternoon and need a little more sedative every night. You're beginning to feel unnecessary too.'

'Am I?' He paused and tried to feel into himself to see what was really there.

'Oh, George!' She looked beyond him, at the nursery door. 'Those lions can't get out of there, can they?'

He looked at the door and saw it tremble as if something had jumped against it from the other side.

'Of course not,' he said.

At dinner they ate alone, for Wendy and Peter were at a special plastic carnival across town and had televised home to say they'd be late, to go ahead eating. So George Hadley, bemused, sat watching the dining-room table produce warm dishes of food from its mechanical interior.

'We forgot the ketchup,' he said.

'Sorry,' said a small voice within the table, and ketchup appeared.

As for the nursery, thought George Hadley, it won't hurt for the children to be locked out of it awhile. Too much of anything isn't good for anyone. And it was clearly indicated that the children had been spending a little too much time on Africa. That *sun*. He could feel it on his neck, still, like a hot paw. And the *lions*. And the smell of blood. Remarkable how the nursery caught the telepathic emanations of the children's minds and created life to fill their every desire. The children thought lions, and there were lions. The children thought zebras, and there were zebras. Sun – sun. Giraffes – giraffes. Death and death.

That last. He chewed tastelessly on the meat that the table had cut for him. Death thoughts. They were awfully young,

Wendy and Peter, for death thoughts. Or, no, you were never too young, really. Long before you knew what death was you were wishing it on someone else. When you were two years old you were shooting people with cap pistols.

But this – the long, hot African veldt – the awful death in the jaws of a lion. And repeated again and again.

'Where are you going?'

He didn't answer Lydia. Preoccupied, he let the lights glow softly on ahead of him, extinguish behind him as he padded to the nursery door. He listened against it. Far away, a lion roared.

He unlocked the door and opened it. Just before he stepped inside, he heard a faraway scream. And then another roar from the lions, which subsided quickly.

He stepped into Africa. How many times in the last year had he opened this door and found Wonderland. Alice, the Mock Turtle, or Aladdin and his Magical Lamp, or Jack Pumpkinhead of Oz, or Dr Doolittle, or the cow jumping over a very real-appearing moon – all the delightful contraptions of a make-believe world. How often had he seen Pegasus flying in the sky ceiling, or seen fountains of red fireworks, or heard angel voices singing. But now, this yellow hot Africa, this bake oven with murder in the heat. Perhaps Lydia was right. Perhaps they needed a little vacation from the fantasy which was growing a bit too real for ten-year-old children. It was all right to exercise one's mind with gymnastic fantasies, but when the lively child mind settled on one pattern … ? It seemed that, at a distance, for the past month, he had heard lions roaring, and smelled their strong odour seeping as far away as his study door. But, being busy, he had paid it no attention.

George Hadley stood on the African grassland alone. The lions looked up from their feeding, watching him. The only flaw to the illusion was the open door through which he could see his wife, far down the dark hall, like a framed picture, eating her dinner abstractedly.

'Go away,' he said to the lions.

They did not go.

He knew the principle of the room exactly. You sent out your thoughts. Whatever you thought would appear.

'Let's have Aladdin and his lamp,' he snapped.

The veldtland remained; the lions remained.

'Come on, room! I demanded Aladdin!' he said.

Nothing happened. The lions mumbled in their baked pelts.

'Aladdin!'

He went back to dinner. 'The fool room's out of order,' he said. 'It won't respond.'

'Or – '

'Or what?'

'Or it *can't* respond,' said Lydia, 'because the children have thought about Africa and lions and killing so many days that the room's in a rut.'

'Could be.'

'Or Peter's set it to remain that way.'

'Set it?'

'He may have got into the machinery and fixed something.'

'Peter doesn't know machinery.'

'He's a wise one for ten. That I.Q. of his – '

'Nevertheless – '

'Hello, Mom. Hello, Dad.'

The Hadleys turned. Wendy and Peter were coming in the front door, cheeks like peppermint candy, eyes like bright blue agate marbles, a smell of ozone on their jumpers from their trip in the helicopter.

'You're just in time for supper,' said both parents.

'We're full of strawberry ice cream and hot dogs,' said the children, holding hands. 'But we'll sit and watch.'

'Yes, come tell us about the nursery,' said George Hadley.

The brother and sister blinked at him and then at each other. 'Nursery?'

'All about Africa and everything,' said the father with false joviality.

'I don't understand,' said Peter.

'Your mother and I were just travelling through Africa with rod and reel; Tom Swift and his Electric Lion,' said George Hadley.

'There's no Africa in the nursery,' said Peter simply.

'Oh, come now, Peter. We know better.'

'I don't remember any Africa,' said Peter to Wendy. 'Do you?'

'No.'

'Run see and come tell.'

She obeyed.

'Wendy, come back here!' said George Hadley, but she was gone. The house lights followed her like a flock of fireflies. Too late, he realized he had forgotten to lock the nursery door after his last inspection.

'Wendy'll look and come tell us,' said Peter.

'She doesn't have to tell *me*. I've seen it.'

'I'm sure you're mistaken, Father.'

'I'm not, Peter. Come along now.'

But Wendy was back. 'It's not Africa,' she said breathlessly.

'We'll see about this,' said George Hadley, and they all walked down the hall together and opened the nursery door.

There was a green, lovely forest, a lovely river, a purple mountain, high voices singing, and Rima, lovely and mysterious, lurking in the trees with colourful flights of butterflies, like animated bouquets, lingering in her long hair. The African veldtland was gone. The lions were gone. Only Rima was here now, singing a song so beautiful that it brought tears to your eyes.

George Hadley looked in at the changed scene. 'Go to bed,' he said to the children.

They opened their mouths.

'You heard me,' he said.

They went off to the air closet, where a wind sucked them like brown leaves up the flue to their slumber rooms.

George Hadley walked through the singing glade and picked up something that lay in the corner near where the lions had been. He walked slowly back to his wife.

'What is that?' she asked.

'An old wallet of mine,' he said.

He showed it to her. The smell of hot grass was on it and the smell of a lion. There were drops of saliva on it, it had been chewed, and there were blood smears on both sides.

He closed the nursery door and locked it, tight.

In the middle of the night he was still awake and he knew his wife was awake. 'Do you think Wendy changed it?' she said at last, in the dark room.

'Of course.'

'Made it from a veldt into a forest and put Rima there instead of lions?'

'Yes.'

'Why?'

'I don't know. But it's staying locked until I find out.'

'How did your wallet get there?'

'I don't know anything,' he said, 'except that I'm beginning to be sorry we bought that room for the children. If children are neurotic at all, a room like that – '

'It's supposed to help them work off their neuroses in a healthful way.'

'I'm starting to wonder.' He stared at the ceiling.

'We've given the children everything they ever wanted. Is this our reward – secrecy, disobedience?'

'Who was it said, "Children are carpets, they should be stepped on occasionally"? We've never lifted a hand. They're insufferable – let's admit it. They come and go when they like; they treat us as if we were offspring. They're spoiled and we're spoiled.'

'They've been acting funny ever since you forbade them to take the rocket to New York a few months ago.'

'They're not old enough to do that alone, I explained.'

'Nevertheless, I've noticed they've been decidedly cool toward us since.'

'I think I'll have David McClean come tomorrow morning to have a look at Africa.'

'But it's not Africa now, it's Green Mansions country* and Rima.'

'I have a feeling it'll be Africa again before then.'

A moment later they heard the screams.

Two screams. Two people screaming from downstairs. And then a roar of lions.

'Wendy and Peter aren't in their rooms,' said his wife.

---

*Green Mansions country: South American rainforest

He lay in his bed with his beating heart. 'No,' he said. 'They've broken into the nursery.'

'Those screams – they sound familiar.'

'Do they?'

'Yes, awfully.'

And although their beds tried very hard, the two adults couldn't be rocked to sleep for another hour. A smell of cats was in the night air.

'Father?' said Peter.

'Yes.'

Peter looked at his shoes. He never looked at his father any more, nor at his mother. 'You aren't going to lock up the nursery for good, are you?'

'That all depends.'

'On what?' snapped Peter.

'On you and your sister. If you intersperse this Africa with a little variety – oh, Sweden perhaps, or Denmark or China – '

'I thought we were free to play as we wished.'

'You are, within reasonable bounds.'

'What's wrong with Africa, Father?'

'Oh, so now you admit you have been conjuring up Africa, do you?'

'I wouldn't want the nursery locked up,' said Peter coldly. 'Ever.'

'Matter of fact, we're thinking of turning the whole house off for about a month. Live sort of a carefree one-for-all existence.'

'That sounds dreadful! Would I have to tie my own shoes instead of letting the shoe tier do it? And brush my own teeth and comb my hair and give myself a bath?'

'It would be fun for a change, don't you think?'

'No, it would be horrid. I didn't like it when you took out the picture painter last month.'

'That's because I wanted you to learn to paint all by yourself, son.'

'I don't want to do anything but look and listen and smell; what else *is* there to do?'

'All right, go play in Africa.'

'Will you shut off the house some time soon?'

'We're considering it.'

'I don't think you'd better consider it any more, Father.'

'I won't have any threats from my son!'

'Very well.' And Peter strolled off to the nursery.

'Am I on time?' said David McClean.

'Breakfast?' asked George Hadley.

'Thanks, had some. What's the trouble?'

'David, you're a psychologist.'

'I should hope so.'

'Well, then, have a look at our nursery. You saw it a year ago when you dropped by; did you notice anything peculiar about it then?'

'Can't say I did; the usual violences, a tendency toward a slight paranoia here or there, usual in children because they feel persecuted by parents constantly, but, oh, really nothing.'

They walked down the hall. 'I locked the nursery up,' explained the father, 'and the children broke back into it during the night. I let them stay so they could form the patterns for you to see.'

There was a terrible screaming from the nursery.

'There it is,' said George Hadley. 'See what you make of it.'

They walked in on the children without rapping.

The screams had faded. The lions were feeding.

'Run outside a moment, children,' said George Hadley. 'No, don't change the mental combination. Leave the walls as they are. Get!'

With the children gone, the two men stood studying the lions clustered at a distance, eating with great relish whatever it was they had caught.

'I wish I knew what it was,' said George Hadley. 'Sometimes I can almost see. Do you think if I brought high-powered binoculars here and – '

David McClean laughed dryly. 'Hardly.' He turned to study all four walls. 'How long has this been going on?'

'A little over a month.'

'It certainly doesn't feel good.'

'I want facts, not feelings.'

'My dear George, a psychologist never saw a fact in his life. He only hears about feelings; vague things. This doesn't feel good, I tell you. Trust my hunches and my instincts. I have a nose for something bad. This is very bad. My advice to you is to have the whole damn room torn down and your children brought to me every day during the next year for treatment.'

'Is it that bad?'

'I'm afraid so. One of the original uses of these nurseries was so that we could study the patterns left on the walls by the child's mind, study at our leisure, and help the child. In this case, however, the room has become a channel toward – destructive thoughts, instead of a release away from them.'

'Didn't you sense this before?'

'I sensed only that you had spoiled your children more than most. And now you're letting them down in some way. What way?'

'I wouldn't let them go to New York.'

'What else?'

'I've taken a few machines from the house and threatened them, a month ago, with closing up the nursery unless they did their homework. I did close it for a few days to show I meant business.'

'Ah, ha!'

'Does that mean anything?'

'Everything. Where before they had a Santa Claus now they have a Scrooge. Children prefer Santas. You've let this room and this house replace you and your wife in your children's affections. This room is their mother and father, far more important in their lives than their real parents. And now you come along and want to shut it off. No wonder there's hatred here. You can feel it coming out of the sky. Feel that sun. George, you'll have to change your life. Like too many others, you've built it around creature comforts. Why, you'd starve tomorrow if something went wrong in your kitchen. You wouldn't know how to tap an egg. Nevertheless, turn everything off. Start new. It'll take time. But we'll make good children out of bad in a year, wait and see.'

'But won't the shock be too much for the children, shutting the room up abruptly, for good?'

'I don't want them going any deeper into this, that's all.'

The lions were finished with their red feast.

The lions were standing on the edge of the clearing watching the two men.

'Now *I'm* feeling persecuted,' said McClean. 'Let's get out of here. I never have cared for these damned rooms. Make me nervous.'

'The lions look real, don't they?' said George Hadley. 'I don't suppose there's any way – '

'What?'

' – that they could *become* real?'

'Not that I know.'

'Some flaw in the machinery, a tampering or something?'

'No.'

They went to the door.

'I don't imagine the room will like being turned off,' said the father.

'Nothing ever likes to die – even a room.'

'I wonder if it hates me for wanting to switch it off?'

'Paranoia is thick around here today,' said David McClean. 'You can follow it like a spoor*. Hello.' He bent and picked up a bloody scarf. 'This yours?'

'No' George Hadley's face was rigid. 'It belongs to Lydia,'

They went to the fuse box together and threw the switch that killed the nursery.

The two children were in hysterics. They screamed and pranced and threw things. They yelled and sobbed and swore and jumped at the furniture.

'You can't do that to the nursery, you can't!'

'Now, children.'

The children flung themselves onto a couch, weeping.

'George,' said Lydia Hadley, 'turn on the nursery, just for a few moments. You can't be so abrupt.'

'No.'

---

*spoor: animal tracks

'You can't be so cruel.'

'Lydia, it's off, and it stays off. And the whole damn house dies as of here and now. The more I see of the mess we've put ourselves in, the more it sickens me. We've been contemplating our mechanical, electronic navels for too long. My God, how we need a breath of honest air!'

And he marched about the house turning off the voice clocks, the stoves, the heaters, the shoe shiners, the shoe lacers, the body scrubbers and swabbers and massagers, and every other machine he could put his hand to.

The house was full of dead bodies, it seemed. It felt like a mechanical cemetery. So silent. None of the humming hidden energy of machines waiting to function at the tap of a button.

'Don't let them do it!' wailed Peter at the ceiling, as if he was talking to the house, the nursery. 'Don't let Father kill everything.' He turned to his father. 'Oh, I hate you!'

'Insults won't get you anywhere.'

'I wish you were dead!'

'We were, for a long while. Now we're going to really start living. Instead of being handled and massaged, we're going to *live*.'

Wendy was still crying and Peter joined her again. 'Just a moment, just one moment, just another moment of nursery,' they wailed.

'Oh George,' said the wife, 'it can't hurt.'

'All right – all right, if they'll only just shut up. One minute, mind you, and then off forever.'

'Daddy, Daddy, Daddy!' sang the children, smiling with wet faces.

'And then we're going on a vacation. David McClean is coming back in half an hour to help us move out and get to the airport. I'm going to dress. You turn the nursery on for a minute, Lydia, just a minute, mind you.'

And the three of them went babbling off while he let himself be vacuumed upstairs through the air flue and set about dressing himself. A minute later Lydia appeared.

'I'll be glad when we get away,' she sighed.

'Did you leave them in the nursery?'

'I wanted to dress too. Oh, that horrid Africa. What can they see in it?'

'Well, in five minutes we'll be on our way to Iowa. Lord, how did we ever get in this house? What prompted us to buy a nightmare?'

'Pride, money, foolishness.'

'I think we'd better get downstairs before those kids get engrossed with those damned beasts again.'

Just then they heard the children calling, 'Daddy, Mommy, come quick – quick!'

They went downstairs in the air flue and ran down the hall. The children were nowhere in sight. 'Wendy? Peter!'

They ran into the nursery. The veldtland was empty save for the lions waiting, looking at them. 'Peter, Wendy?'

The door slammed.

'Wendy, Peter!'

George Hadley and his wife whirled and ran back to the door.

'Open the door!' cried George Hadley, trying the knob. 'Why, they've locked it from the outside! Peter!' He beat at the door. 'Open up!'

He heard Peter's voice outside, against the door.

'Don't let them switch off the nursery and the house,' he was saying.

Mr and Mrs George Hadley beat at the door. 'Now, don't be ridiculous, children. It's time to go. Mr McClean'll be here in a minute and … '

And then they heard the sounds.

The lions on three sides of them, in the yellow veldt grass, padding through the dry straw, rumbling and roaring in their throats.

The lions.

Mr Hadley looked at his wife and they turned and looked back at the beasts edging slowly forward, crouching, tails stiff.

Mr and Mrs Hadley screamed.

And suddenly they realized why those other screams had sounded familiar.

'Well, here I am,' said David McClean in the nursery doorway. 'Oh, hello.' He stared at the two children seated in the centre of the open glade eating a little picnic lunch. Beyond them was the water hole and the yellow veldtland; above was the hot sun. He began to perspire. 'Where are your father and mother?'

The children looked up and smiled. 'Oh, they'll be here directly.'

'Good, we must get going,' At a distance Mr McClean saw the lions fighting and clawing and then quieting down to feed in silence under the shady trees.

He squinted at the lions with his hand up to his eyes.

Now the lions were done feeding. They moved to the water hole to drink.

A shadow flickered over Mr McClean's hot face. Many shadows flickered. The vultures were dropping down the blazing sky.

'A cup of tea?' asked Wendy in the silence.

# Harrison Bergeron
## Kurt Vonnegut, Jr

Like Ray Bradbury's story, *Harrison Bergeron* takes place in the future, and in a domestic setting. New technology is having an important impact on people's lives. The story is told clearly, and with a degree of detachment. But Vonnegut's story explores a different social theme: the idea of what it might mean to make sure that all people were equal. Vonnegut treats the subject with irony and a darkly humorous touch, but the story suggests some serious social questions – about the place of the media in our lives and our freedom to act as individuals.

**Kurt Vonnegut** is an American writer, born in 1922, who often uses features of the science fiction genre in his novels and short stories. *Harrison Bergeron* is from a collection of Vonnegut's short stories called *Welcome to the Monkey House*, which was published in 1968.

The year was 2081, and everybody was finally equal. They weren't only equal before God and the law. They were equal every which way. Nobody was smarter than anybody else. Nobody was better looking than anybody else. Nobody was stronger or quicker than anybody else. All this equality was due to the 211th, 212th, and 213th Amendments to the Constitution, and to the unceasing vigilance of agents of the United States Handicapper General.

Some things about living still weren't quite right, though. April, for instance, still drove people crazy by not being springtime. And it was in that clammy month that the H-G men took George and Hazel Bergeron's fourteen-year-old son, Harrison, away.

It was tragic, all right, but George and Hazel couldn't think about it very hard. Hazel had a perfectly average intelligence, which meant she couldn't think about anything except in short bursts. And George, while his intelligence was way above normal, had a little mental handicap radio in his ear. He was required by law to wear it at all times. It was tuned to a government transmitter. Every twenty seconds or so, the transmitter would send out some sharp noise to keep people like George from taking unfair advantage of their brains.

George and Hazel were watching television. There were tears on Hazel's cheeks, but she'd forgotten for the moment what they were about.

On the television screen were ballerinas.

A buzzer sounded in George's head. His thoughts fled in panic, like bandits from a burglar alarm.

'That was a real pretty dance, that dance they just did,' said Hazel.

'Huh?' said George.

'That dance – it was nice,' said Hazel.

'Yup,' said George. He tried to think a little about the ballerinas. They weren't really very good – no better than anybody else would have been, anyway. They were burdened with sashweights and bags of birdshot, and their faces were masked, so that no one, seeing a free and graceful gesture or a pretty face, would feel like something the cat dragged in. George was toying with the vague notion that maybe dancers shouldn't be handicapped. But he didn't get very far with it before another noise in his ear radio scattered his thoughts.

George winced. So did two out of the eight ballerinas.

Hazel saw him wince. Having no mental handicap herself, she had to ask George what the latest sound had been.

'Sounded like somebody hitting a milk bottle with a ball peen hammer,' said George.

'I'd think it would be real interesting, hearing all the different sounds,' said Hazel, a little envious. 'All the things they think up.'

'Um,' said George.

'Only, if I was Handicapper General, you know what I would do?' said Hazel. Hazel, as a matter of fact, bore a strong resemblance to the Handicapper General, a woman named Diana Moon Glampers. 'If I was Diana Moon Glampers,' said Hazel, 'I'd have chimes on Sunday – just chimes. Kind of in honour of religion.'

'I could think, if it was just chimes,' said George.

'Well – maybe make 'em real loud,' said Hazel. 'I think I'd make a good Handicapper General.'

'Good as anybody else,' said George.

'Who knows better'n I do what normal is?' said Hazel.

'Right,' said George. He began to think glimmeringly about his abnormal son who was now in jail, about Harrison, but a twenty-one-gun salute in his head stopped that.

'Boy!' said Hazel, 'that was a doozy, wasn't it?'

It was such a doozy that George was white and trembling, and tears stood on the rims of his red eyes. Two of the eight ballerinas had collapsed to the studio floor, were holding their temples.

'All of a sudden you look so tired,' said Hazel. 'Why don't you stretch out on the sofa, so's you can rest your handicap bag on the pillows, honeybunch.' She was referring to the forty-seven pounds of birdshot in a canvas bag, which was padlocked around George's neck. 'Go on and rest the bag for a little while,' she said. 'I don't care if you're not equal to me for a while.'

George weighed the bag with his hands. 'I don't mind it,' he said. 'I don't notice it any more. It's just a part of me.'

'You been so tired lately – kind of wore out,' said Hazel. 'If there was just some way we could make a little hole in the bottom of the bag, and just take out a few of them lead balls. Just a few.'

'Two years in prison and two thousand dollars fine for every ball I took out,' said George. 'I don't call that a bargain.'

'If you could just take a few out when you came home from work,' said Hazel. 'I mean – you don't compete with anybody around here. You just sit around.'

'If I tried to get away with it,' said George, 'then other people'd get away with it – and pretty soon we'd be right back to the dark ages again, with everybody competing against everybody else. You wouldn't like that, would you?'

'I'd hate it,' said Hazel.

'There you are,' said George. 'The minute people start cheating on laws, what do you think happens to society?'

If Hazel hadn't been able to come up with an answer to this

question, George couldn't have supplied one. A siren was going off in his head.

'Reckon it'd fall all apart,' said Hazel.

'What would?' said George blankly.

'Society,' said Hazel uncertainly. 'Wasn't that what you just said?'

'Who knows?' said George.

The television programme was suddenly interrupted for a news bulletin. It wasn't clear at first as to what the bulletin was about, since the announcer, like all announcers, had a serious speech impediment. For about half a minute, and in a state of high excitement, the announcer tried to say, 'Ladies and gentlemen – '

He finally gave up, handed the bulletin to a ballerina to read.

'That's all right,' Hazel said of the announcer, 'he tried. That's the big thing. He tried to do the best he could with what God gave him. He should get a nice raise for trying so hard.'

'Ladies and gentlemen – ' said the ballerina, reading the bulletin. She must have been extraordinarily beautiful, because the mask she wore was hideous. And it was easy to see that she was the strongest and most graceful of all the dancers, for her handicap bags were as big as those worn by two-hundred-pound men.

And she had to apologize at once for her voice, which was a very unfair voice for a woman to use. Her voice was a warm, luminous, timeless melody. 'Excuse me – ' she said, and she began again, making her voice absolutely uncompetitive.

'Harrison Bergeron, age fourteen,' she said in a grackle* squawk, 'has just escaped from jail, where he was held on suspicion of plotting to overthrow the government. He is a genius and an athlete, is under-handicapped, and should be regarded as extremely dangerous.'

A police photograph of Harrison Bergeron was flashed on the screen – upside down, then sideways, upside down again, then right side up. The picture showed the full length of Harrison against a background calibrated in feet and inches. He was exactly seven feet tall.

---

*grackle: bird of the jackdaw family

The rest of Harrison's appearance was Halloween and hardware. Nobody had ever borne heavier handicaps. He had outgrown hindrances faster than the H-G men could think them up. Instead of a little ear radio for a mental handicap, he wore a tremendous pair of earphones, and spectacles with thick wavy lenses. The spectacles were intended to make him not only half blind, but to give him whanging headaches besides.

Scrap metal was hung all over him. Ordinarily, there was a certain symmetry, a military neatness to the handicaps issued to strong people, but Harrison looked like a walking junkyard. In the race of life, Harrison carried three hundred pounds.

And to offset his good looks, the H-G men required that he wear at all times a red rubber ball for a nose, keep his eyebrows shaved off, and cover his even white teeth with black caps at snaggle-tooth random.

'If you see this boy,' said the ballerina, 'do not – I repeat, do not – try to reason with him.'

There was the shriek of a door being torn from its hinges.

Screams and barking cries of consternation came from the television set. The photograph of Harrison Bergeron on the screen jumped again and again, as though dancing to the tune of an earthquake.

George Bergeron correctly identified the earthquake, and well he might have – for many was the time his own home had danced to the same crashing tune. 'My God – ' said George, 'that must be Harrison!'

The realization was blasted from his mind instantly by the sound of an automobile collision in his head.

When George could open his eyes again, the photograph of Harrison was gone. A living, breathing Harrison filled the screen.

Clanking, clownish, and huge, Harrison stood in the centre of the studio. The knob of the uprooted studio door was still in his hand. Ballerinas, technicians, musicians, and announcers cowered on their knees before him, expecting to die.

'I am the Emperor!' cried Harrison. 'Do you hear? I am the Emperor! Everybody must do what I say at once!' He stamped his foot and the studio shook.

'Even as I stand here – ' he bellowed, 'crippled, hobbled, sickened – I am a greater ruler than any man who ever lived! Now watch me become what I *can* become!'

Harrison tore the straps of his handicap harness like wet tissue paper, tore straps guaranteed to support five thousand pounds.

Harrison's scrap-iron handicaps crashed to the floor.

Harrison thrust his thumbs under the bar of the padlock that secured his head harness. The bar snapped like celery. Harrison smashed his headphones and spectacles against the wall.

He flung away his rubber-ball nose, revealed a man that would have awed Thor, the god of thunder.

'I shall now select my Empress!' he said, looking down on the cowering people. 'Let the first woman who dares rise to her feet claim her mate and her throne!'

A moment passed, and then a ballerina arose, swaying like a willow.

Harrison plucked the mental handicap from her ear, snapped off her physical handicaps with marvellous delicacy. Last of all, he removed her mask.

She was blindingly beautiful.

'Now – ' said Harrison, taking her hand, 'shall we show the people the meaning of the word dance? Music!' he commanded.

The musicians scrambled back into their chairs, and Harrison stripped them of their handicaps, too. 'Play your best,' he told them, 'and I'll make you barons and dukes and earls.'

The music began. It was normal at first – cheap, silly, false. But Harrison snatched two musicians from their chairs, waved them like batons as he sang the music as he wanted it played. He slammed them back into their chairs.

The music began again and was much improved.

Harrison and his Empress merely listened to the music for a while – listened gravely, as though synchronizing their heartbeats with it.

They shifted their weights to their toes.

Harrison placed his big hands on the girl's tiny waist, letting her sense the weightlessness that would soon be hers.

And then, in an explosion of joy and grace, into the air they sprang!

Not only were the laws of the land abandoned, but the law of gravity and the laws of motion as well.

They reeled, whirled, swivelled, flounced, capered, gambolled, and spun.

They leaped like deer on the moon.

The studio ceiling was thirty feet high, but each leap brought the dancers nearer to it.

It became their obvious intention to kiss the ceiling.

They kissed it.

And then, neutralizing gravity with love and pure will, they remained suspended in air inches below the ceiling, and they kissed each other for a long, long time.

It was then that Diana Moon Glampers, the Handicapper General, came into the studio with a double-barrelled ten-gauge shotgun. She fired twice, and the Emperor and the Empress were dead before they hit the floor.

Diana Moon Glampers loaded the gun again. She aimed it at the musicians and told them they had ten seconds to get their handicaps back on.

It was then that the Bergeron's television tube burned out.

Hazel turned to comment about the blackout to George. But George had gone out into the kitchen for a can of beer.

George came back in with a beer, paused while a handicap signal shook him up. And then he sat down again. 'You been crying?' he said to Hazel.

'Yup,' she said.

'What about?' he said.

'I forget,' she said. 'Something real sad on television.'

'What was it?' he said.

'It's all kind of mixed up in my mind,' said Hazel.

'Forget sad things,' said George.

'I always do,' said Hazel.

'That's my girl,' said George. He winced. There was the sound of a rivetting gun in his head.

'Gee – I could tell that one was a doozy,' said Hazel.

'You can say that again,' said George.

'Gee – ' said Hazel, 'I could tell that one was a doozy.'

# Science Fiction: Activities

## 1 Comparing stories for wide reading

Compare and contrast the extract from H.G. Wells's *The Time Machine* with a twentieth-century science fiction short story. You could choose:
**either**
*The Veldt* by Ray Bradbury
**or**
*Harrison Bergeron* by Kurt Vonnegut, Jr

You might like to comment on:

- The way each story is told.
- The kind of new technology which is described.
- The attitude the writers seem to have to this new technology.
- The settings in which the stories take place.
- The main characters – their jobs, their attitudes, how they are described.
- The vision of the future portrayed in each story.
- The broad social and philosophical questions that the stories explore.
- How these broad questions might relate to the time when the stories were written.

## 2 Opportunities for original writing

When you have thought about what you have learned from studying the stories in this section, write a science fiction story using one of the following ideas:

- Time travel – you could set your story in a future when time travel is as common as catching an aeroplane is today, so that people can take time travel holidays to the future or the past.
- A seemingly innocent piece of new technology, for example answer-phones or voice mail, takes on a life of its own.
- A party of aliens contacts the Prime Minister and asks to make a peaceful diplomatic visit to Earth. What happens when they arrive?
- A story set in a future society where social problems have been 'solved' by electronic tagging of people, curfews and constant surveillance, so that people are forced to stay in their homes.
- A story set in a school, house, prison or hospital of the future.
- A story told through an exchange of e-mail between a writer on one planet and a writer on another planet, or across time between a writer in the future and a writer in the present.

# Section 5
# Horror

Fear is a basic, universal emotion which can either terrify or delight, depending on the circumstances. We might be wrenched awake screaming from our worst nightmare or *choose* to put the frighteners on ourselves by watching a late night horror movie or reading an horrific tale.

This double aspect of horror has given the genre its lasting appeal, all the way from Gothic goings-on in eighteenth-century castles to more contemporary disturbances in suburban houses.

Horror stories are often about people who have over-reached themselves in some way. They have desperately striven for something or someone, but have too easily made moral compromises on the way. Ends have mattered to them more than means. Then they begin the slow, inevitable, terrifying descent into a fate frequently worse than death itself – a hell on earth, awfulness without end.

In a way, horror stories can be seen as warnings about where greed can lead. They often show what happens to people who compromise their moral judgement and allow the obsessive pursuit of personal goals to come before the consideration of others.

As in any genre the trappings, trimmings, codes and conventions are important. The details of the setting, weather, time of day and physical description of the characters all make a difference. The frequent use of science and scientists is interesting, perhaps reflecting fears that many people had, and still have, when faced with the complexities of scientific discovery or new technology.

Animals and certain creatures loom large, sometimes quite literally. A certain way of telling the story which distances readers, holding them at bay, is often noticeable. This can be achieved by using the third person through reports, letters, notes, or the observations of an outsider.

# The Body-Snatcher
## R. L. Stevenson

This classic of the genre was written in 1881 but 'laid aside in justifiable disgust' before publication in a *Christmas Special* some three years later. The fears being explored here are those of death and the dead, with the issue of body-snatching being particularly topical in the early part of the nineteenth century.

The teaching hospitals of the time required a regular supply of human bodies for dissection and anatomical study. Criminal elements were often involved in the supply of cadavers through grave robbing and worse. 1828 saw the infamous trial of Burke and Hare, in which the proprietors of a small Edinburgh boarding house were convicted of murdering fifteen of their guests and selling their bodies for the purposes of scientific dissection.

This story refers directly to that case. Great care has been taken by **R.L.Stevenson** (1850–94) – the author of *Treasure Island* – to create an atmosphere of increasing terror as the story builds to its surprising and dreadful climax. Moral questions concerning greed and the pursuit of personal gain are also clearly at the centre of this terrifying tale.

Every night in the year, four of us sat in the small parlour of the George at Debenham – the undertaker, and the landlord, and Fettes, and myself. Sometimes there would be more; but blow high, blow low, come rain or snow or frost, we four would be each planted in his own particular armchair. Fettes was an old drunken Scotsman, a man of education obviously, and a man of some property, since he lived in idleness. He had come to Debenham years ago, while still young, and by a mere continuance of living had grown to be an adopted townsman. His blue camlet* cloak was a local antiquity, like the church-spire. His

*camlet: woollen cloth

place in the parlour at the George, his absence from church, his old, crapulous*, disreputable vices, were all things of course in Debenham. He had some vague Radical opinions and some fleeting infidelities, which he would now and again set forth and emphasize with tottering slaps upon the table. He drank rum – five glasses regularly every evening; and for the greater portion of his nightly visit to the George sat, with his glass in his right hand, in a state of melancholy alcoholic saturation. We called him the Doctor, for he was supposed to have some special knowledge of medicine, and had been known, upon a pinch, to set a fracture or reduce a dislocation; but, beyond these slight particulars, we had no knowledge of his character and antecedents.

One dark winter night – it had struck nine some time before the landlord joined us – there was a sick man in the George, a great neighbouring proprietor suddenly struck down with apoplexy on his way to Parliament; and the great man's still greater London doctor had been telegraphed to his bedside. It was the first time that such a thing had happened in Debenham, for the railway was but newly open, and we were all proportionately moved by the occurrence.

'He's come,' said the landlord, after he had filled and lighted his pipe.

'He?' said I. 'Who? – not the doctor?'

'Himself,' replied our host.

'What is his name?'

'Dr Macfarlane,' said the landlord.

Fettes was far through his third tumbler, stupidly fuddled, now nodding over, now staring mazily around him; but at the last word he seemed to awaken, and repeated the name 'Macfarlane' twice, quietly enough the first time, but with sudden emotion at the second.

'Yes,' said the landlord, 'that's his name, Doctor Wolfe Macfarlane.'

Fettes became instantly sober; his eyes awoke, his voice became clear, loud, and steady, his language forcible and earnest.

---

*crapulous: drunken

We were all startled by the transformation, as if a man had risen from the dead.

'I beg your pardon,' he said, 'I am afraid I have not been paying much attention to your talk. Who is this Wolfe Macfarlane?' And then, when he had heard the landlord out, 'It cannot be, it cannot be,' he added; 'and yet I would like well to see him face to face.'

'Do you know him, Doctor?' asked the undertaker, with a gasp.

'God forbid' was the reply. 'And yet the name is a strange one; it were too much to fancy two. Tell me, landlord, is he old?'

'Well,' said the host, 'he's not a young man, to be sure, and his hair is white; but he looks younger than you.'

'He is older, though; years older. But,' with a slap upon the table, 'it's the rum you see in my face – rum and sin. This man, perhaps, may have an easy conscience and a good digestion. Conscience! Hear me speak. You would think I was some good, old, decent Christian, would you not? But no, not I; I never canted. Voltaire might have canted if he'd stood in my shoes; but the brains' – with a rattling fillip on his bald head – 'the brains were clear and active, and I saw and made no deductions.'

'If you know this doctor,' I ventured to remark, after a somewhat awful pause, 'I should gather that you do not share the landlord's good opinion.'

Fettes paid no regard to me.

'Yes,' he said, with sudden decision, 'I must see him face to face.'

There was another pause, and then a door was closed rather sharply on the first floor, and a step was heard upon the stair.

'That's the doctor,' cried the landlord. 'Look sharp, and you can catch him.'

It was but two steps from the small parlour to the door of the old George Inn; the wide oak staircase landed almost in the street; there was a room for a Turkey rug and nothing more between the threshold and the last round of the descent; but this little space was every evening brilliantly lit up, not only by the light upon the stair and the great signal-lamp below the sign, but by the warm radiance of the bar-room window. The George thus brightly advertised itself to passers-by in the cold street. Fettes walked steadily to the spot, and we, who were hanging behind, beheld the two men meet, as one of them had phrased it, face to face. Dr Macfarlane was alert and vigorous. His white hair set off his pale and placid, although energetic, countenance. He was richly dressed in the finest of broadcloth and the whitest of linen, with a great gold watchchain, and studs and spectacles of the same precious material. He wore a broad-folded tie, white and speckled with lilac, and he carried on his arm a comfortable driving-coat of fur. There was no doubt but he became his years, breathing, as he did, of wealth and consideration; and it was a surprising contrast to see our parlour sot – bald, dirty, pimpled, and robed in his old camlet cloak – confront him at the bottom of the stairs.

'Macfarlane!' he said somewhat loudly, more like a herald than a friend.

The great doctor pulled up short on the fourth step, as though the familiarity of the address surprised and somewhat shocked his dignity.

'Toddy Macfarlane!' repeated Fettes.

The London man almost staggered. He stared for the swiftest of seconds at the man before him, glanced behind him with a sort of scare, and then in a startled whisper, 'Fettes!' he said, 'you!'

'Ay,' said the other, 'me! Did you think I was dead too? We are not so easy shut of our acquaintance.'

'Hush, hush!' exclaimed the doctor. 'Hush, hush! this meeting is so unexpected – I can see you are unmanned. I hardly knew you, I confess, at first; but I am overjoyed – overjoyed to have this opportunity. For the present it must be how-d'ye-do and good-bye in one, for my fly is waiting, and I must not fail the train; but you shall – let me see – yes – you shall give me your address, and you can count on early news of me. We must do something for you, Fettes. I fear you are out at elbows; but we must see to that for auld lang syne, as once we sang at suppers.'

'Money!' cried Fettes; 'money from you! The money that I had from you is lying where I cast it in the rain.'

Dr Macfarlane had talked himself into some measure of

superiority and confidence, but the uncommon energy of this refusal cast him back into his first confusion.

A horrible, ugly look came and went across his almost venerable countenance. 'My dear fellow,' he said, 'be it as you please; my last thought is to offend you. I would intrude on none. I will leave you my address, however – '

'I do not wish it – I do not wish to know the roof that shelters you,' interrupted the other. 'I heard your name; I feared it might be you; I wished to know if, after all, there were a God; I know now that there is none. Begone!'

He still stood in the middle of the rug, between the stair and the doorway; and the great London physician, in order to escape, would be forced to step to one side. It was plain that he hesitated before the thought of this humiliation. White as he was, there was a dangerous glitter in his spectacles; but while he still paused uncertain, he became aware that the driver of his fly was peering in from the street at this unusual scene and caught a glimpse at the same time of our little body from the parlour, huddled by the corner of the bar. The presence of so many witnesses decided him at once to flee. He crouched together, brushing on the wainscot, and made a dart like a serpent, striking for the door. But his tribulation was not yet entirely at an end, for even as he was passing Fettes clutched him by the arm and these words came in a whisper, and yet painfully distinct, 'Have you seen it again?'

The great rich London doctor cried out aloud with a sharp, throttling cry; he dashed his questioner across the open space, and, with hands over his head, fled out of the door like a detected thief. Before it had occurred to one of us to make a movement, the fly was already rattling toward the station. The scene was over like a dream, but the dream had left proofs and traces of its passage. Next day the servant found the fine gold spectacles broken on the threshold, and that very night we were all standing breathless by the bar-room window, and Fettes at our side, sober, pale, and resolute in look.

'God protect us, Mr Fettes!' said the landlord, coming first into possession of his customary senses. 'What in the universe is all this? These are strange things you have been saying.'

Fettes turned towards us; he looked us each in succession in the face. 'See if you can hold your tongues,' said he. 'That man Macfarlane is not safe to cross; those that have done so already have repented it too late.'

And then, without so much as finishing his third glass, far less waiting for the other two, he bade us good-bye and went forth, under the lamp of the hotel, into the black night.

We three turned to our places in the parlour, with the big red fire and four clear candles; and as we recapitulated what had passed the first chill of our surprise soon changed into a glow of curiosity. We sat late; it was the latest session I have known in the old George. Each man, before we parted, had his theory that he was bound to prove; and none of us had any nearer business in this world than to track out the past of our condemned companion, and surprise the secret that he shared with the great London doctor. It is no great boast, but I believe I was a better hand at working out a story than either of my fellows at the George; and perhaps there is now no other man alive who could narrate to you the following foul and unnatural events.

In his young days Fettes studied medicine in the schools of Edinburgh. He had talent of a kind, the talent that picks up swiftly what it hears and readily retails it for its own. He worked little at home; but he was civil, attentive, and intelligent in the presence of his masters. They soon picked him out as a lad who listened closely and remembered well; nay, strange as it seemed to me when I first heard it, he was in those days well favoured, and pleased by his exterior. There was, at that period, a certain extramural teacher of anatomy, whom I shall here designate by the letter K. His name was subsequently too well known. The man who bore it skulked through the streets of Edinburgh in disguise, while the mob that applauded at the execution of Burke called loudly for the blood of his employer. But Mr K— was then at the top of his vogue; he enjoyed a popularity due partly to his own talent and address, partly to the incapacity of his rival, the university professor. The students, at least, swore by his name, and Fettes believed himself, and was believed by others, to have laid the foundations of success when he had acquired the favour of this meteorically famous man. Mr K—

was a *bon vivant* as well as an accomplished teacher; he liked a sly allusion no less than a careful preparation. In both capacities Fettes enjoyed and deserved his notice, and by the second year of his attendance he held the half-regular position of second demonstrator or sub-assistant in his class.

In this capacity, the charge of the theatre and lecture-room devolved in particular upon his shoulders. He had to answer for the cleanliness of the premises and the conduct of the other students, and it was a part of his duty to supply, receive, and divide the various subjects. It was with a view to this last – at that time very delicate – affair that he was lodged by Mr K— in the same wynd*, and at last in the same building, with the dissecting-rooms. Here, after a night of turbulent pleasures, his hand still tottering, his sight still misty and confused, he would be called out of bed in the black hours before the winter dawn by the unclean and desperate interlopers who supplied the table. He would open the door to these men, since infamous throughout the land. He would help them with their tragic burthen, pay them their sordid price, and remain alone, when they were gone, with the unfriendly relics of humanity. From such a scene he would return to snatch another hour or two of slumber, to repair the abuses of the night, and refresh himself for the labours of the day.

Few lads could have been more insensible to the impressions of a life thus passed among the ensigns of mortality. His mind was closed against all general considerations. He was incapable of interest in the fate and fortunes of another, the slave of his own desires and low ambitions. Cold, light, and selfish in the last resort, he had that modicum of prudence, miscalled morality, which keeps a man from inconvenient drunkenness or punishable theft. He coveted, besides, a measure of consideration from his masters and his fellow-pupils, and he had no desire to fail conspicuously in the external parts of life. Thus he made it his pleasure to gain some distinction in his studies, and day after day rendered unimpeachable eye-service to his employer, Mr K—. For his day of work he indemnified himself

*wynd: narrow alley between houses

by nights of roaring, blackguardly enjoyment; and when that balance had been struck, the organ that he called his conscience declared itself content.

The supply of subjects was a continual trouble to him as well as to his master. In that large and busy class, the raw material of the anatomists kept perpetually running out; and the business thus rendered necessary was not only unpleasant in itself, but threatened dangerous consequences to all who were concerned. It was the policy of Mr K— to ask no questions in his dealings with the trade. 'They bring the boy, and we pay the price.' he used to say, dwelling on the alliteration – '*quid pro quo**.' And, again, and somewhat profanely, 'Ask no questions,' he would tell his assistants, 'for conscience' sake.' There was no understanding that the subjects were provided by the crime of murder. Had that idea been broached to him in words, he would have recoiled in horror; but the lightness of his speech upon so grave a matter was, in itself, an offence against good manners, and a temptation to the men with whom he dealt. Fettes, for instance, had often remarked to himself upon the singular freshness of the bodies. He had been struck again and again by the hangdog, abominable looks of the ruffians who came to him before the dawn; and, putting things together clearly in his private thoughts, he perhaps attributed a meaning too immoral and too categorical to the unguarded counsels of his master. He understood his duty, in short, to have three branches: to take what was brought, to pay the price, and to avert the eye from any evidence of crime.

One November morning this policy of silence was put sharply to the test. He had been awake all night with a racking toothache – pacing his room like a caged beast or throwing himself in fury on his bed – and had fallen at last into that profound, uneasy slumber that so often follows on a night of pain, when he was awakened by the third or fourth angry repetition of the concerted signal. There was a thin, bright moonshine: it was bitter cold, windy, and frosty; the town had

---

**quid pro quo*: (Latin) something exchanged for something of the same value

not yet awakened, but an indefinable stir already preluded the noise and business of the day. The ghouls had come later than usual, and they seemed more than usually eager to be gone. Fettes, sick with sleep, lighted them upstairs. He heard their grumbling Irish voices through a dream; and as they stripped the sack from their sad merchandise he leaned, dozing, with his shoulder propped against the wall; he had to shake himself to find the men their money. As he did so his eyes lighted on the dead face. He started; he took two steps nearer, with the candle raised.

'God Almighty!' he cried. 'That is Jane Galbraith!'

The men answered nothing, but they shuffled nearer the door.

'I know her, I tell you,' he continued. 'She was alive and hearty yesterday. It's impossible she can be dead; it's impossible you should have got this body fairly.'

'Sure, sir, you're mistaken entirely,' said one of the men.

But the other looked Fettes darkly in the eyes, and demanded the money on the spot.

It was impossible to misconceive the threat or to exaggerate the danger. The lad's heart failed him. He stammered some excuses, counted out the sum, and saw his hateful visitors depart. No sooner were they gone than he hastened to confirm his doubts. By a dozen unquestionable marks he identified the girl he had jested with the day before. He saw, with horror, marks upon her body that might well betoken violence. A panic seized him, and he took refuge in his room. There he reflected at length over the discovery that he had made; considered soberly the bearing of Mr K—'s instructions and the danger to himself of interference in so serious a business, and at last, in sore perplexity, determined to wait for the advice of his immediate superior, the class assistant.

This was a young doctor, Wolfe Macfarlane, a high favourite among all the reckless students, clever, dissipated, and unscrupulous to the last degree. He had travelled and studied abroad. His manners were agreeable and a little forward. He was an authority on the stage, skilful on the ice or the links with skate or golf-club; he dressed with nice audacity, and, to put the finishing touch upon his glory, he kept a gig and a strong trotting-horse. With Fettes he was on terms of intimacy; indeed, their relative positions called for some community of life; and when subjects were scarce the pair would drive far into the country in Macfarlane's gig, visit and desecrate some lonely graveyard, and return before dawn with their booty to the door of the dissecting-room.

On that particular morning Macfarlane arrived somewhat earlier than his wont. Fettes heard him, and met him on the stairs, told him his story, and showed him the cause of his alarm. Macfarlane examined the marks on her body.

'Yes,' he said with a nod, 'it looks fishy.'

'Well, what should I do?' asked Fettes.

'Do?' repeated the other. 'Do you want to do anything? Least said soonest mended, I should say.'

'Some one else might recognize her,' objected Fettes 'She was as well known as the Castle Rock.'

'We'll hope not,' said Macfarlane, 'and if anybody does – well, you didn't, don't you see, and there's an end. The fact is, this has been going on too long. Stir up the mud, and you'll get K— into the most unholy trouble; you'll be in a shocking box yourself. So will I, if you come to that. I should like to know how any one of us would look, or what the devil we should have to say for ourselves, in any Christian witness-box. For me, you know there's one thing certain – that, practically speaking, all our subjects have been murdered.'

'Macfarlane!' cried Fettes.

'Come now!' sneered the other. 'As if you hadn't suspected it yourself!'

'Suspecting is one thing – '

'And proof another. Yes, I know; and I'm as sorry as you are this should have come here,' tapping the body with his cane. 'The next best thing for me is not to recognize it; and,' he added coolly, 'I don't. You may, if you please. I don't dictate, but I think a man of the world would do as I do; and I may add, I fancy that is what K— would look for at our hands. The question is, Why did he choose us two for his assistants? And I answer, because he didn't want old wives.'

This was the tone of all others to affect the mind of a lad like

Fettes. He agreed to imitate Macfarlane. The body of the unfortunate girl was duly dissected, and no one remarked or appeared to recognize her.

One afternoon, when his day's work was over, Fettes dropped into a popular tavern and found Macfarlane sitting with a stranger. This was a small man, very pale and dark, with coal-black eyes. The cut of his features gave a promise of intellect and refinement which was but feebly realized in his manners, for he proved, upon a nearer acquaintance, coarse, vulgar, and stupid. He exercised, however, a very remarkable control over Macfarlane; issued orders like the Great Bashaw; became inflamed at the least discussion or delay, and commented rudely on the servility with which he was obeyed. This most offensive person took a fancy to Fettes on the spot, plied him with drinks, and honoured him with unusual confidences on his past career. If a tenth part of what he confessed were true, he was a very loathsome rogue; and the lad's vanity was tickled by the attention of so experienced a man.

'I'm a pretty bad fellow myself,' the stranger remarked, 'but Macfarlane is the boy – Toddy Macfarlane I call him. Toddy, order your friend another glass.' Or it might be, 'Toddy, you jump up and shut the door.' 'Toddy hates me,' he said again. 'Oh, yes, Toddy, you do!'

'Don't you call me that confounded name,' growled Macfarlane.

'Hear him! Did you ever see the lads play knife? He would like to do that all over my body,' remarked the stranger.

'We medicals have a better way than that,' said Fettes. 'When we dislike a dead friend of ours, we dissect him.'

Macfarlane looked up sharply, as though this jest was scarcely to his mind.

The afternoon passed. Gray, for that was the stranger's name, invited Fettes to join them at dinner, ordered a feast so sumptuous that the tavern was thrown in commotion, and when all was done commanded Macfarlane to settle the bill. It was late before they separated; the man Gray was incapably drunk. Macfarlane, sobered by his fury, chewed the cud of the money he had been forced to squander and the slights he had been obliged to swallow. Fettes, with various liquors singing in his head, returned home with devious footsteps and a mind entirely in abeyance. Next day Macfarlane was absent from the class, and Fettes smiled to himself as he imagined him still squiring the intolerable Gray from tavern to tavern. As soon as the hour of liberty had struck he posted from place to place in quest of his last night's companions. He could find them, however, nowhere; so returned early to his rooms, went early to bed, and slept the sleep of the just.

At four in the morning he was awakened by the well-known signal. Descending to the door, he was filled with astonishment to find Macfarlane with his gig, and in the gig one of those long and ghastly packages with which he was so well acquainted.

'What?' he cried. 'Have you been out alone? How did you manage?'

But Macfarlane silenced him roughly, bidding him turn to business. When they had got the body upstairs and laid it on the table, Macfarlane made at first as if he were going away. Then he paused and seemed to hesitate; and then, 'You had better look at the face,' said he, in tones of some constraint. 'You had better,' he repeated, as Fettes only stared at him in wonder.

'But where, and how, and when did you come by it?' cried the other.

'Look at the face,' was the only answer.

Fettes was staggered; strange doubts assailed him. He looked from the young doctor to the body, and then back again. At last, with a start, he did as he was bidden. He had almost expected the sight that met his eyes, and yet the shock was cruel. To see, fixed in the rigidity of death and naked on that coarse layer of sack-cloth, the man whom he had left well-clad and full of meat and sin upon the threshold of a tavern, awoke, even in the thoughtless Fettes, some of the terrors of the conscience. It was a *cras tibi** which re-echoed in his soul, that two whom he had known should have come to lie upon these icy tables. Yet these were only secondary thoughts. His first concern regarded Wolfe. Unprepared for a challenge so

---

**cras tibi*: (Latin) It's your turn tomorrow

momentous, he knew not how to look his comrade in the face. He durst not meet his eye, and he had neither words nor voice at his command.

It was Macfarlane himself who made the first advance. He came up quietly behind and laid his hand gently but firmly on the other's shoulder.

'Richardson,' said he, 'may have the head.'

Now Richardson was a student who had long been anxious for that portion of the human subject to dissect. There was no answer, and the murderer resumed: 'Talking of business, you must pay me; your accounts, you see, must tally.'

Fettes found a voice, the ghost of his own: 'Pay you!' he cried. 'Pay you for that?'

'Why, yes, of course you must. By all means and on every possible account, you must,' returned the other. 'I dare not give it for nothing, you dare not take it for nothing; it would compromise us both. This is another case like Jane Galbraith's. The more things are wrong the more we must act as if all were right. Where does old K— keep his money?'

'There,' answered Fettes hoarsely, pointing to a cupboard in the corner.

'Give me the key, then,' said the other, calmly, holding out his hand.

There was an instant's hesitation, and the die was cast. Macfarlane could not suppress a nervous twitch, the infinitesimal mark of an immense relief, as he felt the key between his fingers. He opened the cupboard, brought out pen and ink and a paper-book that stood in one compartment, and separated from the funds in a drawer a sum suitable to the occasion.

'Now, look here,' he said, 'there is the payment made – first proof of your good faith: first step to your security. You have now to clinch it by a second. Enter the payment in your book, and then you for your part may defy the devil.'

The next few seconds were for Fettes an agony of thought; but in balancing his terrors it was the most immediate that triumphed. Any future difficulty seemed almost welcome if he could avoid a present quarrel with Macfarlane. He set down the candle which he had been carrying all the time, and with a steady hand entered the date, the nature, and the amount of the transaction.

'And now,' said Macfarlane, 'it's only fair that you should pocket the lucre*. I've had my share already. By-the-by, when a man of the world falls into a bit of luck, has a few shillings extra in his pocket – I'm ashamed to speak of it, but there's a rule of conduct in the case. No treating, no purchase of expensive class-books, no squaring of old debts; borrow, don't lend.'

'Macfarlane,' began Fettes, still somewhat hoarsely, 'I have put my neck in a halter to oblige you.'

'To oblige me?' cried Wolfe. 'Oh, come! You did, as near as I can see the matter, what you downright had to do in self-defence. Suppose I got into trouble, where would you be? This second little matter flows clearly from the first. Mr Gray is the continuation of Miss Galbraith. You can't begin and then stop. If you begin, you must keep on beginning; that's the truth. No rest for the wicked.'

A horrible sense of blackness and the treachery of fate seized hold upon the soul of the unhappy student.

'My God!' he cried, 'but what have I done? and when did I begin? To be made a class assistant – in the name of reason, where's the harm in that? Service wanted the position; Service might have got it. Would *he* have been where *I* am now?'

'My dear fellow,' said Macfarlane, 'what a boy you are! What harm *has* come to you? What harm *can* come to you if you hold your tongue? Why, man, do you know what this life is? There are two squads of us – the lions and the lambs. If you're a lamb, you'll come to lie upon these tables like Gray or Jane Galbraith; if you're a lion, you'll live and drive a horse like me, like K—, like all the world with any wit or courage. You're staggered at the first. But look at K—! My dear fellow, you're clever, you have pluck. I like you, and K— likes you. You were born to lead the hunt; and I tell you, on my honour and my experience of life, three days from now you'll laugh at all these scarecrows like a high-school boy at a farce.'

And with that Macfarlane took his departure and drove off

---

*lucre: money

up the wynd in his gig to get under cover before daylight. Fettes was thus left alone with his regrets. He saw the miserable peril in which he stood involved. He saw, with inexpressible dismay, that there was no limit to his weakness, and that, from concession to concession, he had fallen from the arbiter of Macfarlane's destiny to his paid and helpless accomplice. He would have given the world to have been a little braver at the time, but it did not occur to him that he might still be brave. The secret of Jane Galbraith and the cursed entry in the day-book closed his mouth.

Hours passed; the class began to arrive; the members of the unhappy Gray were dealt out to one and to another, and received without remark. Richardson was made happy with the head; and before the hour of freedom rang Fettes trembled with exultation to perceive how far they had already gone toward safety.

For two days he continued to watch, with increasing joy, the dreadful process of disguise.

On the third day Macfarlane made his appearance. He had been ill, he said; but he made up for lost time by the energy with which he directed the students. To Richardson in particular he extended the most valuable assistance and advice, and that student, encouraged by the praise of the demonstrator, burned high with ambitious hopes, and saw the medal already in his grasp.

Before the week was out Macfarlane's prophecy had been fulfilled. Fettes had outlived his terrors and had forgotten his baseness. He began to plume himself upon his courage, and had so arranged the story in his mind that he could look back on these events with an unhealthy pride. Of his accomplice he saw but little. They met, of course, in the business of the class; they received their orders together from Mr K—. At times they had a word or two in private, and Macfarlane was from first to last particularly kind and jovial. But it was plain that he avoided any reference to their common secret; and even when Fettes whispered to him that he had cast in his lot with the lions and foresworn the lambs, he only signed to him smilingly to hold his peace.

At length an occasion arose which threw the pair once more into a closer union. Mr K— was again short of subjects; pupils were eager, and it was a part of this teacher's pretensions to be always well supplied. At the same time there came the news of a burial in the rustic graveyard of Glencorse. Time has little changed the place in question. It stood then, as now, upon a cross-road, out of call of human habitations, and buried fathom deep in the foliage of six cedar trees. The cries of the sheep upon the neighbouring hills, the streamlets upon either hand, one loudly singing among pebbles, the other dripping furtively from pond to pond, the stir of the wind in mountainous old flowering chestnuts, and once in seven days the voice of the bell and the old tunes of the precentor*, were the only sounds that disturbed the silence around the rural church. The Resurrection Man – to use a by-name of the period – was not to be deterred by any of the sanctities of customary piety. It was part of his trade to despise and desecrate the scrolls and trumpets of old tombs, the paths worn by the feet of worshippers and mourners, and the offerings and the inscriptions of bereaved affection. To rustic neighbourhoods, where love is more than commonly tenacious, and where some bonds of blood or fellowship unite the entire society of a parish, the body-snatcher, far from being repelled by natural respect, was attracted by the ease and safety of the task. To bodies that had been laid in earth, in joyful expectation of a far different awakening, there came that hasty, lamp-lit, terror-haunted resurrection of the spade and mattock. The coffin was forced, the cerements* torn, and the melancholy relics, clad in sackcloth, after being rattled for hours on moonless by-ways, were at length exposed to uttermost indignities before a class of gaping boys.

Somewhat as two vultures may swoop upon a dying lamb, Fettes and Macfarlane were to be let loose upon a grave in that green and quiet resting-place. The wife of a farmer, a woman who had lived for sixty years, and been known for nothing but

---

*precentor: person who leads the singing in a church
*cerements: grave-clothes

good butter and a godly conversation, was to be rooted from her grave at midnight and carried, dead and naked, to that faraway city that she had always honoured with her Sunday best; the place beside her family was to be empty till the crack of doom; her innocent and almost venerable members to be exposed to that last curiosity of the anatomist.

Late one afternoon the pair set forth, well wrapped in cloaks and furnished with a formidable bottle. It rained without remission – a cold, dense, lashing rain. Now and again there blew a puff of wind, but these sheets of falling water kept it down. Bottle and all, it was a sad and silent drive as far as Penicuik, where they were to spend the evening. They stopped once, to hide their implements in a thick bush not far from the churchyard, and once again at the Fisher's Tryst, to have a toast before the kitchen fire and vary their nips of whisky with a glass of ale. When they reached their journey's end the gig was housed, the horse was fed and comforted, and the two young doctors in a private room sat down to the best dinner and the best wine the house afforded. The lights, the fire, the beating rain upon the window, the cold, incongruous work that lay before them, added zest to their enjoyment of the meal. With every glass their cordiality increased. Soon Macfarlane handed a little pile of gold to his companion.

'A compliment,' he said. 'Between friends these little d—d accommodations ought to fly like pipe-lights.'

Fettes pocketed the money, and applauded the sentiment to the echo. 'You are a philosopher,' he cried. 'I was an ass till I knew you. You and K— between you, by the Lord Harry! but you'll make a man of me.'

'Of course we shall,' applauded Macfarlane. 'A man? I tell you, it required a man to back me up the other morning. There are some big, brawling, forty-year-old cowards who would have turned sick at the look of the d—d thing; but not you – you kept your head. I watched you.'

'Well, and why not?' Fettes thus vaunted himself. 'It was no affair of mine. There was nothing to gain on the one side but disturbance, and on the other I could count on your gratitude, don't you see?' And he slapped his pocket till the gold pieces rang.

Macfarlane somehow felt a certain touch of alarm at these unpleasant words. He may have regretted that he had taught his young companion so successfully, but he had no time to interfere, for the other noisily continued in this boastful strain:

'The great thing is not to be afraid. Now, between you and me, I don't want to hang – that's practical; but for all cant, Macfarlane, I was born with a contempt. Hell, God, Devil, right, wrong, sin, crime, and all the old gallery of curiosities – they may frighten boys, but men of the world, like you and me, despise them. Here's to the memory of Gray!'

It was by this time growing somewhat late. The gig, according to order, was brought round to the door with both lamps brightly shining, and the young men had to pay their bill and take the road. They announced that they were bound for Peebles, and drove in that direction till they were clear of the last houses of the town; then, extinguishing the lamps, returned upon their course, and followed a by-road toward Glencorse. There was no sound but that of their own passage, and the incessant, strident pouring of the rain. It was pitch dark; here and there a white gate or a white stone in the wall guided them for a short space across the night; but for the most part it was at a foot pace, and almost groping, that they picked their way through that resonant blackness to their solemn and isolated destination. In the sunken woods that traverse the neighbourhood of the burying-ground the last glimmer failed them, and it became necessary to kindle a match and reillumine one of the lanterns of the gig. Thus, under the dripping trees, and environed* by huge and moving shadows, they reached the scene of their unhallowed labours.

They were both experienced in such affairs, and powerful with the spade; and they had scarce been twenty minutes at their task before they were rewarded by a dull rattle on the coffin lid. At the same moment Macfarlane, having hurt his hand upon a stone, flung it carelessly above his head. The grave, in which they now stood almost to the shoulders, was

---

*environed: surrounded

close to the edge of the plateau of the graveyard; and the gig lamp had been propped, the better to illuminate their labours, against a tree, and on the immediate verge of the steep bank descending to the stream. Chance had taken a sure aim with the stone. Then came a clang of broken glass; night fell upon them; sounds alternately dull and ringing announced the bounding of the lantern down the bank, and its occasional collision with the trees. A stone or two, which it had dislodged in its descent, rattled behind it into the profundities of the glen; and then silence, like night, resumed its sway; and they might bend their hearing to its utmost pitch, but naught was to be heard except the rain, now marching to the wind, now steadily falling over miles of open country.

They were so nearly at an end of their abhorred task that they judged it wisest to complete it in the dark. The coffin was exhumed and broken open; the body inserted in the dripping sack and carried between them to the gig; one mounted to keep it in its place, and the other, taking the horse by the mouth, groped along by wall and bush until they reached the wider road by the Fisher's Tryst. Here was a faint, diffused radiancy, which they hailed like daylight; by that they pushed the horse to a good pace and began to rattle along merrily in the direction of the town.

They had both been wetted to the skin during their operations, and now, as the gig jumped among the deep ruts, the thing that stood propped between them fell now upon one and now upon the other. At every repetition of the horrid contact each instinctively repelled it with greater haste; and the process, natural although it was, began to tell upon the nerves of the companions. Macfarlane made some ill-favoured jest about the farmer's wife, but it came hollowly from his lips, and was allowed to drop in silence. Still their unnatural burthen bumped from side to side; and now the head would be laid, as if in confidence, upon their shoulders, and now the drenching sackcloth would flap icily about their faces. A creeping chill began to possess the soul of Fettes. He peered at the bundle, and it seemed somehow larger than at first. All over the countryside, and from every degree of distance, the farm dogs accompanied their passage with tragic ululations*; and it grew and grew upon his mind that some unnatural miracle had been accomplished, that some nameless change had befallen the dead body, and that it was in fear of their unholy burden that the dogs were howling.

'For God's sake,' said he, making a great effort to arrive at speech, 'for God's sake, let's have a light!'

Seemingly Macfarlane was affected in the same direction; for though he made no reply, he stopped the horse, passed the reins to his companion, got down, and proceeded to kindle the remaining lamp. They had by that time got no farther than the cross-road down to Auchendinny. The rain still poured as though the deluge were returning, and it was no easy matter to make a light in such a world of wet and darkness. When at last the flickering blue flame had been transferred to the wick and began to expand and clarify, and shed a wide circle of misty brightness round the gig, it became possible for the two young men to see each other and the thing they had along with them. The rain had moulded the rough sacking to the outlines of the body underneath; the head was distinct from the trunk, the shoulders plainly modelled; something at once spectral and human riveted their eyes upon the ghastly comrade of their drive.

For some time Macfarlane stood motionless, holding up the lamp. A nameless dread was swathed, like a wet sheet, about the body, and tightened the white skin upon the face of Fettes; a fear that was meaningless, a horror of what could not be, kept mounting to his brain. Another beat of the watch, and he had spoken. But his comrade forestalled him.

'That is not a woman,' said Macfarlane, in a hushed voice.

"It was a woman when we put her in,' whispered Fettes.

'Hold that lamp,' said the other. 'I must see her face.'

And as Fettes took the lamp his companion untied the fastenings of the sack and drew down the cover from the head. The light fell very clear upon the dark, well-moulded features and smooth-shaven cheeks of a too familiar countenance, often

---

*ululations: howling

beheld in dreams of both of these young men. A wild yell rang up into the night; each leaped from his own side into the roadway; the lamp fell, broke, and was extinguished; and the horse, terrified by this unusual commotion, bounded and went off toward Edinburgh at a gallop, bearing along with it, sole occupant of the gig, the body of the dead and long-dissected Gray.

# The Quest for 'Blank Claveringi'

## Patricia Highsmith

This story combines a number of the elements discussed in the introduction to the horror genre. An ambitious scientist, a professor of zoology in this case, is determined to make a name for himself and is not averse to cutting a few corners in the process.

A rare species of giant man-eating snail is apparently to be found on the remote tropical island of Kuwa. A hasty, solo expedition is mounted, but a series of basic errors means that very soon things start to go dreadfully wrong. As the tension builds and as we move towards the all too inevitable conclusion, we are left asking the most basic of questions – why?

**Patricia Highsmith** (1921–95), an American writer who later moved to France, is perhaps best known for her first novel *Strangers on a Train* which was made into a famous film by another master of horror and suspense – Alfred Hitchcock. *The Quest for 'Blank Claveringi'* was first published in 1972, in a collection of her short stories called *Eleven*.

Avery Clavering, a professor of zoology at a California university, heard of the giant snails of Kuwa in a footnote of a book on molluscs. His sabbatical* had been coming up in three months when he read the few lines:

> It is said by Matusas Islands natives that snails even larger than this exist on the uninhabited island of Kuwa, twenty-five miles distant from the Matusas. The Matusans claim that these snails have a shell diameter of twenty feet and that they are man-eating. Dr Wm. J. Stead, now living in the Matusas, visited Kuwa in 1949 without finding any snails at all, but the legend persists.

*sabbatical: study leave

The item aroused Professor Clavering's interest, because he very much wanted to discover some animal, bird, reptile or even mollusc to which he could give his name, *Something-or-other Claveringi*. The professor was forty-eight. His time, perhaps, was not growing short, but he had achieved no particular renown. The discovery of a new species would win him immortality in his field.

The Matusas, the professor saw on a map, were three small islands arranged like the points of an isosceles triangle not far from Hawaii. He wrote a letter to Dr Stead and received the following reply, written on an abominable typewriter, so many words pale, he could scarcely read it:

April 8th, 19–

Dear Professor Clavering:

I have long heard of the giant snails of Kuwa, but before you make a trip of such length, I must tell you that the natives here assure me a group of them went about twenty years ago to Kuwa to exterminate these so-called man-eating snails which they imagined would swim the ocean between Kuwa and the Matusas and do some damage to the latter islands. They claim to have killed off the whole community of them except for one old fellow they could not kill. This is typical of native stories – there's always one that got away. I haven't much doubt the snails were no bigger than three feet across and that they were not —— (here a word was illegible, due both to the pale ribbon and a squashed insect). You say you read of my effort in 1949 to find the giant snails. What the footnote did not say is that I have made several trips since to find them. I retired to the Matusas, in fact, for that purpose. I now believe the snails to be mere folklore, a figment of the natives' imagination. If I were you, I would not waste time or money on an expedition.

Yours sincerely,
Wm. J. Stead, M.D.

Professor Clavering had the money and the time. He detected a sourness in Dr Stead's letter. Maybe Dr Stead had just had bad luck. By post, Professor Clavering hired a thirty-foot sail-boat with an auxiliary motor from Hawaii. He wanted to make the trip alone from the Matusas. *Blank Claveringi*. Regardless of the size, the snail was apt to be different from any known snail, because of its isolation – if it existed. He planned to go one month ahead of his wife and to join her and their twenty-year-old daughter Wanda in Hawaii for a more orthodox holiday after he had visited Kuwa. A month would give him plenty of time to find the snail, even if there were only one to take photographs, and make notes.

It was late June when Professor Clavering, equipped with water tanks, tinned beef, soup and milk, biscuits, writing materials, camera, knife, hatchet and a Winchester .22 which he hardly knew how to use, set forth from one of the Matusas bound for Kuwa. Dr Stead, who had been his host for a few days, saw him off. Dr Stead was seventy-five, he said, but he looked older, due perhaps to the ravages of drink and the apparently aimless life he led now. He had not looked for the giant snail in two years, he said.

'I've given the last third of my life to looking for this snail, you might say,' Dr Stead added. 'But that's man's fate, I suppose, the pursuit of the non-existent. Well – good luck to you, Professor Clavering!' He waved his old American straw hat as the *Samantha* left the dock under motor power.

Professor Clavering had made out to Stead that if he did find snails, he would come back at once, get some natives to accompany him, and return to Kuwa with materials to make crates for the snails. Stead had expressed doubt whether he could persuade any natives to accompany him, if the snail or snails were really large. But then, Dr Stead had been negative about everything pertaining to Professor Clavering's quest. Professor Clavering was glad to get away from him.

After about an hour, Professor Clavering cut the motor and tentatively hoisted some sail. The wind was favourable, but he knew little about sails, and he paid close attention to his compass. At last, Kuwa came into view, a tan hump on a sea of blue. He was quite close before he saw any greenery, and this was only the tops of some trees. Already, he was looking for anything resembling a giant snail, and regretting he had not brought binoculars, but the island was only three miles long and one mile broad. He decided to aim for a small beach. He dropped anchor, two of them, in water so clear he could see the sand under it. He stood for a few minutes on the deck.

The only life he saw was a few birds in the tops of trees, brightly coloured, crested birds, making cries he had never heard before. There was no low-lying vegetation whatsoever, none of the grass and reeds that might have been expected on an island such as this – much like the Matusas in soil-colour – and this augured well for the presence of snails that might have devoured everything green within their reach. It was only a quarter to two. Professor Clavering ate part of a papaya, two boiled eggs, and brewed coffee on his alcohol burner, as he had had nothing to eat since 6 a.m. Then with his hunting knife and hatchet in the belt of his khaki shorts, and his camera around his neck, he lowered himself into the water. The *Samantha* carried no rowboat.

He sank up to his neck, but he could walk on the bottom. He held the camera high. He emerged panting, as he was some twenty pounds overweight. Professor Clavering was to regret every one of those pounds before the day was over, but as he got his breath and looked around him, and felt himself drying off in the warm sunlight, he was happy. He wiped his hatchet and knife with dry sand, then walked inland, alert for the rounded form of a snail's shell, moving or stationary, anywhere. But as snails were more or less nocturnal, he thought any snails might well be sleeping in some cave or crevice with no idea of emerging until nightfall.

He decided to cross the island first, then follow the coast to right or left and circle the island. He had not gone a quarter of a mile, when his heart gave a leap. Ten yards before him, he saw three bent saplings with their top leaves chewed off. The young trees were four inches in diameter at their bases. It would have taken a considerable weight to bend them down, something like a hundred pounds. The professor looked on the trees and the ground for the glaze left by snails, but found none. But rain could have washed it away. A snail whose shell was three foot in diameter could not weigh enough to bend such a tree, so Professor Clavering now hoped for something bigger. He pushed on.

He arrived at the other side of the island. The sea had eaten a notch into the shore, forming a mostly dry gulley of a hundred yards' length and a depth of thirty feet. The land here was sandy but moist, and there was, he saw, a little vegetation in the form of patchy grass. But here, the lower branches of all the trees had been divested of their leaves, and so long ago that the branches had dried and fallen off. All this bespoke the presence of land snails. Professor Clavering stooped and looked down into the gulley. He saw, just over the edge of the crevice, the pink-tan curve of something that was neither rock nor sand. If it was a snail, it was monstrous. Involuntarily, he took a step backward, scattering pebbles down the gulley.

The professor ran round the gulley to have a better look. It was a snail, and its shell was about fifteen feet high. He had a view of its left side, the side without the spiral. It resembled a peach-coloured sail filled with wind, and the sunlight made nacreous*, silvery patches gleam and twinkle as the great thing stirred. The little rain of pebbles had aroused it, the professor realized. If the shell was fifteen or eighteen feet in diameter, he reckoned that the snail's body or foot would be something like six yards long when extended. Rooted to the spot, the professor stood, thrilled as much by the (as yet) empty phrase *Blank Claveringi* which throbbed in his head as by the fact that he was looking upon something no man had seen before, or at least no scientist. The crate would have to be bigger than he had thought, but the *Samantha* would be capable of taking it on her forward deck.

The snail was backing to pull its head from the narrow part of the gulley. The moist body, the colour of tea with milk, came into view with the slowness of an enormous snake awakening from slumber. All was silent, except for pebbles dropping from the snail's underside as it lifted its head, except for the professor's constrained breathing. The snail's head, facing

---

*nacreous: pearly

inland, rose higher and higher, and its antennae, with which it saw, began to extend. Professor Clavering realized he had disturbed it from its diurnal* sleep, and a brief terror caused him to retreat again, sending more pebbles down the slope.

The snail heard this, and slowly turned its enormous head towards him.

The professor felt paralysed. A gigantic face regarded him, a face with drooping, scalloped cheeks or lips, with antennae six feet long now, the eyes on the ends of them scrutinizing him at his own level and scarcely ten feet away, with the disdain of a Herculean lorgnette*, with the unknown potency of a pair of oversized telescopes. The snail reared so high, it had to arch its antennae to keep him in view. Six yards long? It would be more like eight or ten yards. The snail turned itself to move towards him.

Still, the professor did not budge. He knew about snails' teeth, the twenty-odd thousand pairs of them even in a small garden snail, set in comblike structures, the upper front teeth visible, moving up and down constantly just under the transparent flesh. A snail of this size, with proportionate teeth, could chew through a tree as quickly as a woodsman's axe, the professor thought. The snail was advancing up the bank with monumental confidence. He had to stand still for a few seconds simply to admire it. *His* snail! The professor opened his camera and took a picture, just as the snail was hauling its shell over the edge of the quarry.

'You are magnificent!' Professor Clavering said in a soft and awestruck voice. Then he took a few steps backward.

It was pleasant to think he could skip nimbly about, comparatively speaking, observing the snail from all angles, while the snail could only creep towards him at what seemed the rate of one yard in ten seconds. The professor thought to watch the snail for an hour or so, then go back to the *Samantha* and write some notes. He would sleep aboard the boat, take some more photographs tomorrow morning, then

---

*diurnal: daytime

*lorgnette: spectacles on a long handle

start under engine power back to the Matusas. He trotted for twenty yards, then turned to watch the snail approach.

The snail travelled with its head lifted three feet above the ground, keeping the professor in the focus of its eyes. It was moving faster. Professor Clavering retreated sooner than he intended, and before he could get another picture.

Now Professor Clavering looked around for a mate of the snail. He was rather glad not to see another snail, but he cautioned himself not to rule out the possibility of a mate. It wouldn't be pleasant to be cornered by two snails, yet the idea excited him. Impossible to think of a situation in which he could not escape from two slow, lumbering creatures like the – the what? *Amygdalus Persica* (his mind stuck on peaches, because of the beautiful colour of the shell) *Carnivora* (perhaps) *Claveringi*. That could be improved upon, the professor thought as he walked backward, watching.

A little grove of trees gave him an idea. If he stood in the grove, the snail could not reach him, and he would also have a close view. The professor took a stand amid twelve or fifteen trees, all about twenty feet high. The snail did not slacken its speed, but began to circle the grove, still watching the professor. Finding no opening big enough between two trees, the snail raised it head higher, fifteen feet high, and began to creep up on the trees. Branches cracked, and one tree snapped.

Professor Clavering ducked and retreated. He had a glimpse of a great belly gliding unhurt over a jagged tree trunk, of a circular mouth two feet across, open and showing the still wider upper band of teeth like shark's teeth, munching automatically up and down. The snail cruised gently down over the tree tops, some of which sprang back into position as the snail's weight left them.

*Click!* went the professor's camera.

What a sight that had been! Something like a slow hurdle. He imagined entertaining friends with an account of it, substantiated by the photograph, once he got back to California. Old Professor McIlroy of the biology department had laughed at him for spending seven thousand dollars on an effort he predicted would be futile!

Professor Clavering was tiring, so he cut directly for the *Samantha*. He noticed that the snail veered also in a direction that would intercept him, if they kept on at their steady though different speeds, and the professor chuckled and trotted for a bit. The snail also picked up speed, and the professor remembered the wide, upward rippling of the snail's body as it had hurdled the trees. It would be interesting to see how fast the snail could go on a straight course. Such a test would have to wait for America.

He reached the water and saw his beach a few yards away to his right, but no ship was there. He'd made a mistake, he thought, and his beach was on the other side of the island. Then he caught sight of the *Samantha* half a mile out on the ocean, drifting away.

'*Damn!*' Professor Clavering said aloud. He'd done something wrong with the anchors. Did he dare try to swim to it? The distance frightened him, and it was growing wider every moment.

A rattle of pebbles behind him made him turn. The snail was hardly twenty feet away.

The professor trotted down towards the beach. There was bound to be some slit on the coast, a cave however small, where he could be out of reach of the snail. He wanted to rest for a while. What really annoyed him now was the prospect of a chilly night without blankets or food. The Matusas natives had been right: there was nothing to eat on Kuwa.

Professor Clavering stopped dead, his shoes sliding on sand and pebbles. Before him, not fifty feet away on the beach, was another snail as big as the one following him, and somewhat lighter in colour. Its tail was in the sea, and its muzzle dripped water as it reared itself to get a look at him.

It was this snail, the professor realized, that had chewed through the hemp ropes and let the boat go free. Was there something about new hemp ropes that appealed to snails? This question he put out of his mind for the nonce*. He had a snail before and behind him. The professor trotted on along the

---

*for the nonce: for the time being

shore. The only crevice of shelter he was sure existed was the gulley on the other side of the island. He forced himself to walk at a moderate pace for a while, to breathe normally, then he sat down and treated himself to a rest.

The first snail was the first to appear, and as it had lost sight of him, it lifted its head and looked slowly to right and left, though without slackening its progress. The professor sat motionless, bare head lowered, hoping the snail would not see him. But he was not that lucky. The snail saw him and altered its course to a straight line for him. Behind it came the second snail – its wife? its husband? – the professor could not tell and there was no way of telling.

Professor Clavering had to leave his resting place. The weight of his hatchet reminded him that he at least had a weapon. A good scare, he thought, a minor wound might discourage them. He knew they were hungry, that their teeth could tear his flesh more easily than they tore trees, and that alive or dead, he would be eaten by these snails, if he permitted it to happen. He drew his hatchet and faced them, conscious that he cut a not very formidable figure with his slight paunch, his pale, skinny legs, his height of five feet seven, about a third the snails' height, but his brows above his glasses were set with a determination to defend his life.

The first snail reared when it was ten feet away. The professor advanced and swung the hatchet at the projecting mantle on the snail's left side. He had not dared get close enough, his aim was inches short, and the weight of the hatchet pulled the professor off balance. He staggered and fell under the raised muzzle, and had just time to roll himself from under the descending mouth before it touched the ground where he had been. Angry now, he circled the snail and swung a blow at the nacreous shell, which turned the blade. The hatchet took an inch-deep chip, but nothing more. The professor swung again, higher this time and in the centre of the shell's posterior, trying for the lung valve beneath, but the valve was still higher, he knew, ten feet from the ground, and once more his hatchet took only a chip. The snail began to turn itself to face him.

The professor then confronted the second snail, rushed at it and swung the hatchet, cutting it in the cheek. The hatchet sank up to its wooden handle, and he had to tug to get it out, and then had to run a few yards, as the snail put on speed and reared its head for a biting attack. Glancing back, the professor saw that no liquid (he had not, of course, expected blood) came from the cut in the snail's cheek, and in fact he couldn't see the cut. And the blow had certainly been no discouragement to the snail's advance.

Professor Clavering began to walk at a sensible pace straight for the snails' lair on the other side of the island. By the time he scrambled down the side of the gulley, he was winded and his legs hurt. But he saw to his relief that the gulley narrowed to a sharp V. Wedged in that, he would be safe. Professor Clavering started into the V, which had an overhanging top rather like a cave, when he saw that what he had taken for some rounded rocks were moving – at least some of them were. They were baby snails! They were larger than good-sized beach balls. And the professor saw, from the way a couple of them were devouring grass blades, that they were hungry.

A snail's head appeared high on his left. The giant parent snail began to descend the gulley. A crepitation*, a pair of antennae against the sky on his right, heralded the arrival of the second snail. He had nowhere to turn except the sea, which was not a bad idea, he thought, as these were land snails. The professor waded out and turned left, walking waist-deep in water. It was slow going, and a snail was coming after him. He got closer to the land and ran in thigh-deep water.

The first snail, the darker one, entered the water boldly and crept along in a depth of several inches, showing signs of being willing to go into deeper water when it got abreast of Professor Clavering. The professor hoped the other snail, maybe the mother, had stayed with the young. But it hadn't. It was following along the land, and accelerating. The professor plunged wildly for the shore where he would be able to move faster.

*crepitation: grating sound

Now, thank goodness, he saw rocks. Giant igneous masses of rocks covered a sloping hill down to the sea. There was bound to be a niche, some place there where he could take shelter. The sun was sinking into the ocean, it would be dark soon, and there was no moon, he knew. The professor was thirsty. When he reached the rocks, he flung himself like a corpse into a trough made by four or five scratchy boulders, which caused him to lie in a curve. The rocks rose two feet above his body, and the trough was hardly a foot wide. A snail couldn't, he reasoned, stick its head down here and bite him.

The peachy curves of the snails' shells appeared, and one, the second, drew closer.

'I'll strike it with my hatchet if it comes!' the professor swore to himself. 'I'll cut its face to ribbons with my knife!' He was now reconciled to killing both adults, because he could take back a pair of the young ones, and in fact more easily because they were smaller.

The snail seemed to sniff like a dog, though inaudibly, as its muzzle hovered over the professor's hiding place. Then with majestic calm it came down on the rocks between which the professor lay. Its slimy foot covered the aperture and within seconds had blocked out almost all the light.

Professor Clavering drew his hunting knife in anger and panic, and plunged it several times into the snail's soft flesh. The snail seemed not even to wince. A few seconds later, it stopped moving, though the professor knew that it was not only not dead, as the stabs hadn't touched any vital organs, but that it had fastened itself over his trench in the firmest possible way. No slit of light showed. The professor was only grateful that the irregularity of the rocks must provide a supply of air. Now he pressed frantically with his palms against the snail's body, and felt his hands slip and scrape against rock. The firmness of the snail, his inability to budge it, made him feel slightly sick for a moment.

An hour passed. The professor almost slept, but the experience was more like a prolonged hallucination. He dreamed, or feared, that he was being chewed by twenty thousand pairs of teeth into a heap of mince, which the two giant snails shared with their offspring. To add to his misery, he was cold and hungry. The snail's body gave no warmth, and was even cool.

Some hours later, the professor awoke and saw stars above him. The snail had departed. It was pitch dark. He stood up cautiously, trying not to make a sound, and stepped out of the crevice. He was free! On a sandy stretch of beach a few yards away, Professor Clavering lay down, pressed against a vertical face of rock. Here he slept the remaining hours until dawn.

He awakened just in time, and perhaps not the dawn but a sixth sense had awakened him. The first snail was coming towards him and was only ten feet away. The professor got up on trembling legs, and trotted inland, up a slope. An idea came to him: if he could push a boulder of, say, five hundred pounds – possible with a lever – on to an adult snail in the gulley and smash the spot below which its lungs lay, then he could kill it. Otherwise, he could think of no other means at his disposal that could inflict a fatal injury. His gun might, but the gun was on the *Samantha*. He had already estimated that it might be a week, or never, that help would come from the Matusas. The *Samantha* would not necessarily be seen by any ship for days, and even if was seen, would it be apparent she was drifting? And if so, would the spotters make a bee-line for the Matusas to report it? Not necessarily. The professor bent quickly and licked some dew from a leaf. The snails were twenty yards behind him now.

*The trouble is, I'm becoming exhausted*, he said to himself.

He was even more tired at noon. Only one snail pursued him, but the professor imagined the other resting or eating a tree top, in order to be fresh later. The professor could trot a hundred yards, find a spot to rest in, but he dared not shut his eyes for long, lest he sleep. And he was definitely weak from lack of food.

So the day passed. His idea of dropping a rock down the gulley was thwarted by two factors: the second snail was guarding the gulley now, at the top of its V, and there was no such rock as he needed within a hundred yards.

When dusk came, the professor could not find the hill where the igneous rocks were. Both snails had him in their sight now.

His watch said a quarter to seven. Professor Clavering took a deep breath and faced the fact that he must make an attempt to kill one or both snails before dark. Almost without thinking, or planning – he was too spent for that – he chopped down a slender tree and hacked off its branches. The leaves of these branches were devoured by the two snails five minutes after the branches had fallen to the ground. The professor dragged his tree several yards inland, and sharpened one end of it with the hatchet. It was too heavy a weapon for one hand to wield, but in two hands, it made a kind of battering ram, or giant spear.

At once, Professor Clavering turned and attacked, running with the spear pointed slightly upward. He aimed for the first snail's mouth, but struck too low, and the tree end penetrated about four inches into the snail's chest – or the area below its face. No vital organ here, except the long, straight œsophagus, which in these giant snails would be set deeper than four inches. He had nothing for his trouble but lacerated hands. His spear hung for a few seconds in the snail's flesh, then fell out on to the ground. The professor retreated, pulling his hatchet from his belt. The second snail, coming up abreast of the other, paused to chew off a few inches of the tree stump, then joined its mate in giving attention to Professor Clavering. There was something contemptuous, something absolutely assured, about the snails' slow progress towards him, as if they were thinking. 'Escape us a hundred, a thousand times, we shall finally reach you and devour every trace of you.'

The professor advanced once more, circled the snail he had just hit with the tree spear, and swung the hatchet at the rear of its shell. Desperately, he attacked the same spot with five or six direct hits, for now he had a plan. His hacking operation had to be halted, because the second snail was coming up behind him. Its snout and an antenna even brushed the professor's legs moistly and staggered him, before he could step out of its way. Two more hatchet blows the professor got in, and then he stopped because his right arm hurt. He had by no means gone through the shell, but he had no strength for more effort with the hatchet. He went back for his spear. His target was a small one, but he ran towards it with desperate purpose.

The blow landed. It even broke through.

The professor's hands were further torn, but he was oblivious of them. His success made him as joyous as if he had killed both his enemies, as if a rescue ship with food, water, and a bed were even then sailing into Kuwa's beach.

The snail was twisting and rearing up with pain.

Professor Clavering ran forward, lifted the drooping spear and pushed it with all his might farther into the snail, pointing it upwards to go as close as possible to the lung. Whether the snail died soon or not, it was *hors de combat**, the professor saw. And he himself experienced something like physical collapse an instant after seeing the snail's condition. He was quite incapable of taking on the other snail in the same manner, and the other snail was coming after him. The professor tried to walk in a straight line away from both snails, but he weaved with fatigue and faintness. He looked behind him. The unhurt snail was thirty feet away. The wounded snail faced him, but was motionless, half in and half out of its shell, suffering in silence some agony of asphyxiation. Professor Clavering walked on.

Quite by accident, just as it was growing dark, he came upon his field of rocks. Among them he took shelter for the second time. The snail's snout probed the trench in which he lay, but could not quite reach him. Would it not be better to remain in the trench tomorrow, to hope for rain for water? He fell asleep before he could come to any decision.

Again, when the professor awakened at dawn, the snail had departed. His hands throbbed. Their palms were encrusted with dried blood and sand. He thought it wise to go to the sea and wash them in salt water.

The giant snail lay between him and the sea, and at his approach, the snail very slowly began to creep towards him. Professor Clavering made a wobbling detour and continued on his way towards the water. He dipped his hands and moved them rapidly back and forth, at last lifted water to his face, longed to wet his dry mouth, warned himself that he should not, and yielded anyway, spitting out the water almost at once.

---

**hors de combat*: (French) disabled

Land snails hated salt and could be killed by salt crystals. The professor angrily flung handfuls of water at the snail's face. The snail only lifted its head higher, out of the professor's range. Its form was slender now, and it had, oddly, the grace of a horned gazelle, of some animal of the deer family. The snail lowered its snout, and the professor trudged away, but not quickly enough: the snail came down on his shoulder and the suctorial mouth clamped.

The professor screamed. *My God*, he thought, as a piece of his shirt, a piece of flesh and possibly bone was torn from his left shoulder, *why was I such an ass as to linger*? The snail's weight pushed him under, but it was shallow here, and he struggled to his feet and walked towards the land. Blood streamed hotly down his side. He could not bear to look at his shoulder to see what had happened, and would not have been surprised if his left arm had dropped off in the next instant. The professor walked on aimlessly in shallow water near the land. He was still going faster than the snail.

Then he lifted his eyes to the empty horizon, and saw a dark spot in the water in the mid-distance. He stopped, wondering if it were real or a trick of his eyes: but now he made out the double body of a catamaran, and he thought he saw Dr Stead's straw hat. They had come from the Matusas!

'Hello!' The professor was shocked at the hoarseness, the feebleness of his voice. Not a chance that he had been heard.

But with hope now, the professor's strength increased. He headed for a little beach – not his beach, a smaller one – and when he got there he stood in its centre, his good arm raised, and shouted. 'Dr *Stead*! This way – On the beach!' He could definitely see Dr Stead's hat and four dark heads.

There was no answering shout. Professor Clavering could not tell if they had heard him or not. And the accursed snail was only thirty feet away now! He'd lost his hatchet, he realized. And the camera that had been under water with him was now ruined, and so were the two pictures in it. No matter. He would live.

'*Here!*' he shouted, again lifting his arm.

The natives heard this. Suddenly all heads in the catamaran turned to him.

Dr Stead pointed to him and gesticulated, and dimly Professor Clavering heard the good doctor urging the boatman to make for the shore. He saw Dr Stead half stand up in the catamaran.

The natives gave a whoop – at first Professor Clavering thought it a whoop of joy, or of recognition, but almost at once a wild swing of the sail, a splash of oars, told him that the natives were trying to change their course.

Pebbles crackled. The snail was near. And this of course was what the natives had seen – the giant snail.

'*Please – Here!*' the professor screamed. He plunged again into the water. '*Please!*'

Dr Stead was trying, that the professor could see. But the natives were rowing, paddling with hands even, and their sail was carrying them obliquely away.

The snail made a splash as it entered the sea. To drown or to be eaten alive? the professor wondered. He was waist-deep when he stumbled, waist-deep but head under when the snail crashed down upon him, and he realised as the thousands of pairs of teeth began to gnaw at his back that his fate was both to drown and to be chewed to death.

# The Lottery
## Shirley Jackson

This is a truly shocking twentieth-century short story. On the surface everything is calm and orderly. A small community is preparing for an annual event – a lottery – in an organized and rational way. No voices are raised in anger, but gradually, step by nervous step, we realize that all is not exactly as it seems. The ending, when it finally hits us, is simply unforgettable.

Without giving away too much of the plot, moral questions are most definitely at stake in this story. When fundamental moral issues are brought into question, for whatever reason, then we begin again that long, inevitable and ultimately terrifying descent into horror.

When the American novelist **Shirley Jackson** (1919-65) wrote this story for the *New Yorker* magazine in 1948, panicked readers responded in record numbers. Stephen King has written recently of Shirley Jackson that 'the more quietly she speaks, the more terrifying she is, and the closer we lean in to listen'.

The morning of June 27th was clear and sunny, with the fresh warmth of a full-summer day; the flowers were blossoming profusely and the grass was richly green. The people of the village began to gather in the square, between the post office and the bank, around ten o'clock; in some towns there were so many people that the lottery took two days and had to be started on June 26th, but in this village, where there were only about three hundred people, the whole lottery took less than two hours, so it could begin at ten o'clock in the morning and still be through in time to allow the villagers to get home for noon dinner.

The children assembled first, of course. School was recently over for the summer, and the feeling of liberty sat uneasily on most of them; they tended to gather together quietly for a while before they broke into boisterous play, and their talk was still of the classroom and the teacher, of books and reprimands. Bobby Martin had already stuffed his pockets full of stones, and the other boys soon followed his example, selecting the smoothest and roundest stones; Bobby and Harry Jones and Dick Delacroix – the villagers pronounced this name 'Dellacroy' – eventually made a great pile of stones in one corner of the square and guarded it against the raids of the other boys. The girls stood aside, talking among themselves, looking over their shoulders at the boys, and the very small children rolled in the dust or clung to the hands of their older brothers or sisters.

Soon the men began to gather, surveying their own children, speaking of planting and rain, tractors and taxes. They stood together, away from the pile of stones in the corner, and their jokes were quiet and they smiled rather than laughed. The women, wearing faded house dresses and sweaters, came shortly after their menfolk. They greeted one another and exchanged bits of gossip as they went to join their husbands. Soon the women, standing by their husbands, began to call to their children, and the children came reluctantly, having to be called four or five times. Bobby Martin ducked under his mother's grasping hand and ran, laughing, back to the pile of stones. His father spoke up sharply, and Bobby came quickly and took his place between his father and his oldest brother.

The lottery was conducted – as were the square dances, the teenage club, the Halloween program – by Mr Summers, who had time and energy to devote to civic activities. He was a round-faced, jovial man and he ran the coal business, and people were sorry for him, because he had no children and his wife was a scold. When he arrived in the square, carrying the black wooden box, there was a murmur of conversation among the villagers, and he waved and called, 'Little late today, folks.' The postmaster, Mr Graves, followed him, carrying a three-legged stool, and the stool was put in the center of the square and Mr Summers set the black box down on it. The villagers kept their distance, leaving a space between themselves and the stool, and when Mr Summers said, 'Some of you fellows want to give me a hand?' there was a hesitation before two men, Mr Martin and his oldest son, Baxter, came forward to hold the box steady on the stool while Mr Summers stirred up the papers inside it.

The original paraphernalia for the lottery had been lost long ago, and the black box now resting on the stool had been put into use even before Old Man Warner, the oldest man in town, was born. Mr Summers spoke frequently to the villagers about making a new box, but no one liked to upset even as much tradition as was represented by the black box. There was a story that the present box had been made with some pieces of the box that had preceded it, the one that had been constructed when the first people settled down to make a village here. Every year, after the lottery, Mr Summers began talking again about a new box, but every year the subject was allowed to fade off without anything's being done. The black box grew shabbier each year; by now it was no longer completely black but splintered badly along one side to show the original wood color, and in some places faded or stained.

Mr Martin and his oldest son, Baxter, held the black box securely on the stool until Mr Summers had stirred the papers thoroughly with his hand. Because so much of the ritual had been forgotten or discarded, Mr Summers had been successful in having slips of paper substituted for the chips of wood that had been used for generations. Chips of wood, Mr Summers had argued, had been all very well when the village was tiny, but now that the population was more than three hundred and likely to keep growing, it was necessary to use something that would fit more easily into the black box. The night before the lottery, Mr Summers and Mr Graves made up the slips of paper and put them in the box, and it was then taken to the safe of Mr Summers' coal company and locked up until Mr Summers was ready to take it to the square next morning. The rest of the year, the box was put away, sometimes one place, sometimes another; it had spent one year in Mr Graves' barn and another year underfoot in the post office, and sometimes it was set on a shelf in the Martin grocery and left there.

There was a great deal of fussing to be done before Mr Summers declared the lottery open. There were lists to make up – of heads of families, heads of households in each family, members of each household in each family. There was the proper swearing-in of Mr Summers by the postmaster, as the official of the lottery; at one time, some people remembered, there had been a recital of some sort, performed by the official of the lottery, a perfunctory, tuneless chant that had been rattled off duly each year; some people believed that the official of the lottery used to stand just so when he said or sang it, others believed that he was supposed to walk among the people, but years and years ago this part of the ritual had been allowed to lapse. There had been, also, a ritual salute, which the official of the lottery had to use in addressing each person who came up to draw from the box, but this also had changed with time, until now it was felt necessary only for the official to speak to each person approaching. Mr Summers was very good at all this; in his clean white shirt and blue jeans, with one hand resting carelessly on the black box, he seemed very proper and important as he talked interminably to Mr Graves and the Martins.

Just as Mr Summers finally left off talking and turned to the assembled villagers, Mrs Hutchinson came hurriedly along the path to the square, her sweater thrown over her shoulders, and slid into place in the back of the crowd. 'Clean forgot what day it was,' she said to Mrs Delacroix, who stood next to her, and they both laughed softly. 'Thought my old man was out back stacking wood,' Mrs Hutchinson went on, 'and then I looked out the window and the kids was gone, and then I remembered it was the twenty-seventh and camea-running.' She dried her hands on her apron, and Mrs Delacroix said, 'You're in time, though. They're still talking away up there.'

Mrs Hutchinson craned her neck to see through the crowd and found her husband and children standing near the front.

She tapped Mrs Delacroix on the arm as a farewell and began to make her way through the crowd. The people separated good-humoredly to let her through; two or three people said, in voices just loud enough to be heard across the crowd, 'Here comes your Missus, Hutchinson,' and 'Bill, she made it after all.'

Mrs Hutchinson reached her husband, and Mr Summers, who had been waiting, said cheerfully, 'Thought we were going to have to get on without you, Tessie.' Mrs Hutchinson said, grinning, 'Wouldn't have me leave m'dishes in the sink, now, would you, Joe?', and soft laughter ran through the crowd as the people stirred back into position after Mrs Hutchinson's arrival.

'Well, now,' Mr Summers said soberly, 'guess we better get started, get this over with, so's we can go back to work. Anybody ain't here?'

'Dunbar,' several people said. 'Dunbar, Dunbar.'

Mr Summers consulted his list. 'Clyde Dunbar,' he said. 'That's right. He's broke his leg, hasn't he? Who's drawing for him?'

'Me, I guess,' a woman said, and Mr Summers turned to look at her. 'Wife draws for her husband,' Mr Summers said. 'Don't you have a grown boy to do it for you, Janey?' Although Mr Summers and everyone else in the village knew the answer perfectly well, it was the business of the official of the lottery to ask such questions formally. Mr Summers waited with an expression of polite interest while Mrs Dunbar answered.

'Horace's not but sixteen yet,' Mrs Dunbar said regretfully. 'Guess I gotta fill in for the old man this year.'

'Right,' Mr Summers said. He made a note on the list he was holding. Then he asked, 'Watson boy drawing this year?'

A tall boy in the crowd raised his hand. 'Here,' he said. 'I'm drawing for m'mother and me.' He blinked his eyes nervously and ducked his head as several voices in the crowd said things like 'Good fellow, Jack,' and 'Glad to see your mother's got a man to do it.'

'Well,' Mr Summers said, 'guess that's everyone. Old Man Warner make it?'

'Here,' a voice said, and Mr Summers nodded.

A sudden hush fell on the crowd as Mr Summers cleared his throat and looked at the list. 'All ready?' he called. 'Now, I'll read the names – heads of families first – and the men come up and take a paper out of the box. Keep the paper folded in your hand without looking at it until everyone has had a turn. Everything clear?'

The people had done it so many times that they only half listened to the directions; most of them were quiet, wetting their lips, not looking around. Then Mr Summers raised one hand high and said, 'Adams.' A man disengaged himself from the crowd and came forward. 'Hi, Steve,' Mr Summers said, and Mr Adams said, 'Hi, Joe.' They grinned at one another humorlessly and nervously. Then Mr Adams reached into the black box and took out a folded paper. He held it firmly by one corner as he turned and went hastily back to his place in the crowd, where he stood a little apart from his family, not looking down at his hand.

'Allen,' Mr Summers said. 'Anderson. Bentham.'

'Seems like there's no time at all between lotteries any more,' Mrs Delacroix said to Mrs Graves in the back row. 'Seems like we got through with the last one only last week.'

'Time sure goes fast,' Mrs Graves said.

'Clark … Delacroix.'

'There goes my old man,' Mrs Delacroix said. She held her breath while her husband went forward.

'Dunbar,' Mrs Summers said, and Mrs Dunbar went steadily to the box while one of the women said, 'Go on, Janey,' and another said, 'There she goes.'

'We're next,' Mrs Graves said. She watched while Mr Graves came around from the side of the box, greeted Mr Summers gravely, and selected a slip of paper from the box. By now, all through the crowd there were men holding the small folded papers in their large hands, turning them over and over nervously. Mrs Dunbar and her two sons stood together. Mrs Dunbar holding the slip of paper.

'Harburt … Hutchinson.'

'Get up there, Bill,' Mrs Hutchinson said, and the people near her laughed.

'Jones.'

'They do say,' Mr Adams said to Old Man Warner, who stood next to him, 'that over in the north village they're talking of giving up the lottery.'

Old Man Warner snorted. 'Pack of crazy fools,' he said. 'Listening to the young folks, nothing's good enough for *them*.

Next thing you know, they'll be wanting to go back to living in caves, nobody work any more, live *that* way for a while. Used to be a saying about "Lottery in June, corn be heavy soon". First thing you know, we'd all be eating stewed chickweed and acorns. There's *always* been a lottery,' he added petulantly. 'Bad enough to see young Joe Summers up there joking with everybody.

'Some places have already quit lotteries,' Mrs Adams said.

'Nothing but trouble in *that*,' Old Man Warner said stoutly. 'Pack of young fools.'

'Martin.' And Bobby Martin watched his father go forward. 'Overdyke ... Percy.'

'I wish they'd hurry,' Mrs Dunbar said to her older son. 'I wish they'd hurry.'

'They're almost through,' her son said.

'You get ready to run tell Dad,' Mrs Dunbar said.

Mr Summers called his own name and then stepped forward precisely and selected a slip from the box. Then he called, 'Warner.'

'Seventy-seventh year I been in the lottery,' Old Man Warner said as he went through the crowd. 'Seventy-seventh time.'

'Watson,' The tall boy came awkwardly through the crowd. Someone said, 'Don't be nervous, Jack,' and Mr Summers said, 'Take your time, son.'

'Zanini.'

After that, there was a long pause, a breathless pause, until Mr Summers, holding his slip of paper in the air, said, 'All right, fellows.' For a minute, no one moved, and then all the slips of paper were opened. Suddenly, all the women began to speak at once, saying, 'Who is it?', 'Who's got it?', 'Is it the Dunbars?', 'Is it the Watsons?' Then the voices began to say, 'It's Hutchinson. It's Bill ... Bill Hutchinson's got it.'

'Go tell your father,' Mrs Dunbar said to her older son.

People began to look around to see the Hutchinsons. Bill Hutchinson was standing quiet, staring down at the paper in his hand. Suddenly, Tessie Hutchinson shouted to Mr Summers, 'You didn't give him time enough to take any paper he wanted. I saw you. It wasn't fair!'

'Be a good sport, Tessie,' Mrs Delacroix called, and Mrs Graves said, 'All of us took the same chance.'

'Shut up, Tessie,' Bill Hutchinson said.

'Well, everyone,' Mr Summers said, 'that was done pretty fast, and now we've got to be hurrying a little more to get done in time.' He consulted his next list. 'Bill,' he said, 'you draw for the Hutchinson family. You got any other households in the Hutchinsons?'

'There's Don and Eva,' Mrs Hutchinson yelled. 'Make them take their chance!'

'Daughters draw with their husbands' families, Tessie,' Mr Summers said gently. 'You know that as well as anyone else.'

'It wasn't *fair*,' Tessie said.

'I guess not, Joe,' Bill Hutchinson said regretfully. 'My daughter draws with her husband's family, that's only fair. And I've got no other family except the kids.'

'Then, as far as drawing for families is concerned, it's you,' Mr Summers said in explanation, 'and as far as drawing for households is concerned, that's you, too. Right?'

'Right,' Bill Hutchinson said.

'How many kids, Bill?' Mr Summers asked formally.

'Three,' Bill Hutchinson said. 'There's Bill, Jr, and Nancy, and little Dave. And Tessie and me.'

'All right, then, Mr Summers said. 'Harry, you got their tickets back?'

Mr Graves nodded and held up the slips of paper. 'Put them in the box, then,' Mr Summers directed. 'Take Bill's and put it in.'

'I think we ought to start over,' Mrs Hutchinson said, as quietly as she could. 'I tell you it wasn't *fair*. You didn't give him time enough to choose. Everybody saw that.'

Mr Graves had selected the five slips and put them in the box, and he dropped all the papers but those on to the ground, where the breeze caught them and lifted them off.

'Listen, everybody,' Mrs Hutchinson was saying to the people around her.

'Ready, Bill?' Mr Summers asked, and Bill Hutchinson, with one quick glance around at his wife and children, nodded.

'Remember,' Mr Summers said, 'take the slips and keep

them folded until each person has taken one. Harry, you help little Dave.' Mr Graves took the hand of the little boy, who came willingly with him up to the box. 'Take a paper out of the box, Davy,' Mr Summers said. Davy put his hand into the box and laughed. 'Take just one paper,' Mr Summers said. 'Harry, you hold it for him.' Mr Graves took the child's hand and removed the folded paper from the tight fist and held it while little Dave stood next to him and looked up at him wonderingly.

'Nancy next,' Mr Summers said. Nancy was twelve, and her schoolfriends breathed heavily as she went forward, switching her skirt, and took a slip daintily from the box. 'Bill, Jr,' Mr Summers said, and Billy, his face red and his feet over-large, nearly knocked the box over as he got a paper out. 'Tessie,' Mr Summers said. She hesitated for a minute, looking around defiantly, and then set her lips and went up to the box. She snatched a paper out and held it behind her.

'Bill,' Mr Summers said, and Bill Hutchinson reached into the box and felt around, bringing his hand out at last with the slip of paper in it.

The crowd was quiet. A girl whispered, 'I hope it's not Nancy,' and the sound of the whisper reached the edges of the crowd.

'It's not the way it used to be,' Old Man Warner said clearly. 'People ain't the way they used to be.'

'All right,' Mr Summers said. 'Open the papers. Harry, you open little Dave's.'

Mr Graves opened the slip of paper and there was a general sigh through the crowd as he held it up and everyone could see that it was blank. Nancy and Bill, Jr, opened theirs at the same time, and both beamed and laughed, turning around to the crowd and holding their slips of paper above their heads.

'Tessie,' Mr Summers said. There was a pause, and then Mr Summers looked at Bill Hutchinson, and Bill unfolded his paper and showed it. It was blank.

'It's Tessie,' Mr Summers said, and his voice was hushed. 'Show us her paper, Bill.'

Bill Hutchinson went over to his wife and forced the slip of paper out of her hand. It had a black spot on it, the black spot Mr Summers had made the night before with the heavy pencil in the coal-company office. Bill Hutchinson held it up, and there was a stir in the crowd.

'All right, folks,' Mr Summers said. 'Let's finish quickly.'

Although the villagers had forgotten the ritual and lost the original black box, they still remembered to use stones. The pile of stones the boys had made earlier was ready; there were stones on the ground with the blowing scraps of paper that had come out of the box. Mrs Delacroix selected a stone so large she had to pick it up with both hands and turned to Mrs Dunbar. 'Come on,' she said. 'Hurry up.'

Mrs Dunbar had small stones in both hands, and she said, gasping for breath, 'I can't run at all. You'll have to go ahead and I'll catch up with you.'

The children had stones already, and someone gave little Davy Hutchinson a few pebbles.

Tessie Hutchinson was in the center of a cleared space by now, and she held her hands out desperately as the villagers moved in on her. 'It isn't fair,' she said. A stone hit her on the side of the head.

Old Man Warner was saying, 'Come on, come on, everyone.' Steve Adams was in the front of the crowd of villagers with Mrs Graves beside him.

'It isn't fair, it isn't right,' Mrs Hutchinson screamed, and then they were upon her.

# Serena Sees

## G. K. Sprinkle

*Serena Sees* is a contemporary horror story set in the high-tech world of radio. An anxious broadcaster with a new studio technician is giving advice on a late night talk show – 'She gives people what they want; nothing wrong with that.' Or is there? Why is she so bothered by the persistent caller? She has the technology – hasn't she?

**G. K. Sprinkle** is a psychiatric counsellor specializing in family violence. She lives in Texas and *Serena Sees* is her first published story.

Barbara inhaled deeply, awareness seeping through the trance. If only she could come back from her meditations to those who wanted her, instead of also facing station politics and sceptics. Snatches of sounds emanated from the headphones around her neck. She opened her eyes, scanning the studio equipment. One phone line was blinking. The CRT showed all four lines open, three breaks before eleven.

'The new guy's on this hour,' the producer said through her desk speaker. 'I'll be back before midnight.'

She looked up through the glass separating radio studio from control room. 'No.'

'It's okay, I've briefed him,' he said. 'Seen those ratings? We're number one this time slot.' He held his right thumb up. 'Checked your abort/delay switch?'

She smiled and nodded. He left. They were a great team. She entertained; he promoted. She brought her lips to the microphone, 'Testing, one … two … three.' She looked into the control room. The new tech nodded, and flashed ten fingers twice. 'Go ahead, use the desk speaker,' she said. She put the headphones on. Perfect timing. The eerie music the producer liked ended.

'There are things beyond sight. Things beyond sound.

Things in the dark reaches of the mind that few can see.' Barbara hated the deep bass voice-over. 'She lights the way … Serena.' The music crescendoed; cymbals crashed.

'Good evening,' Barbara said. 'Welcome to Serena Sees. Your questions answered Monday through Friday from ten until one. All phone lines are open, 387-KNTE. Your problems, your questions; I want to help. Call 387-KNTE.' She looked at the CRT – no Dave, Ed, or Al, thank God, but he did keep changing his name – Mary on the first line. She pushed it. 'Hello Mary. You're on the air with Serena. Can I help?'

'Hello Serena. It's so good to talk with you. I listen all the time. You're wonderful.'

'Thank you Mary. Let me help you.' Good, a talker. Should be easy.

'Oh, I'm praying you can. Will my husband find a job?'

Barbara sighed. These calls tore her apart. People wanting advice instead of fun. 'He's been out of work a while,' she tried.

'Yes. Six months. They say he's too old.'

God, he'd probably never get another job. 'I see a job in his future, but not soon. I feel he'll be starting a business of his own.'

'But he was a telephone lineman.'

That was a toughie. 'He's always wanted to do something else.'

'Yes. How did you know he wanted to raise chickens?'

'Serena sees. Thank you for calling. Our lines are open for your questions, 387-KNTE. Hello, Jack, you're on with Serena Sees. Your question.' Please, not him, she thought.

'Yes. I wonder about my future.'

Someone new, good. 'The future is cloudy, the more I know the better.' That should bring him out.

'Will my girl take me back?'

'I see pain, harsh words between you.'

'Yes.'

He was a clam, but maybe … 'She wants to get married; you don't.'

'No.'

'She's worried about money.' Please. Talk.

'I thought so. Fraud.'

Oops. She pushed the abort/delay switch. 'We don't say things like that on Serena Sees,' she said. Thank God for delays; no one would know what he said. 'More of Serena Sees after these messages. Our lines are open; 387-KNTE.'

Barbara sipped water as the commercials droned in her ears. Her hands shook slightly. Why did it bother her so much this time? She gave people what they wanted; nothing wrong with that. No, it wasn't the last caller. It was the other one with the cold, quiet voice. That Dave or Ed or Al, or whatever his name was. What did he want? Why did he call?

'Five seconds,' the new tech whispered through the desk speaker.

'Speak louder,' she said. 'It's okay.' Barbara leaned toward the microphone. The commercial ended. 'It's so good to be back. Our lines are open for you – 387-KNTE. Hello, Don, you're on with Serena Sees. Your question.'

'What do you see in *your* future, Barbara?'

No, not that voice, four nights in a row. She didn't see the new guy in the booth. She pushed the abort switch. How did that caller get through?

He laughed. 'Don't know, do you psychic? You told Cindy I was wrong for her, and you know nothing about us.'

The call didn't disconnect. Barbara jiggled the headphones – dead. He was talking through the desk speaker. She plugged her headphone into another jack. The 10.30 news tape was running. She pushed a phone line and dialled 911. Nothing happened. The lights went off. She felt a cold draft as the door to the hall opened behind her.

# Horror: Activities

## 1 Comparing stories for wide reading

Compare and contrast the way tension is built and a sense of horror achieved in:
*The Body-Snatcher* by R. L. Stevenson and
**either**
*The Quest for 'Blank Claveringi'* by Patricia Highsmith
**or**
*The Lottery* by Shirley Jackson
**or**
*Serena Sees* by G. K. Sprinkle

You might like to comment on:

- The importance of the setting and the atmosphere generated within each story.
- The way the central characters are described.
- Other specific ways in which language is used for effect.
- The use of science and technology, and the role of scientists in the stories.
- The seemingly inevitable way in which the events unfold.
- The shape of the stories.
- Some of the moral questions raised by the stories.
- The nature of the horror achieved by the stories.

## 2 Opportunities for original writing

After reflecting on what you have learned from studying the stories in this section, write about:

- An incident set in the past which retains the power to shock us to this day.
- A story set in a remote or exotic location which turns into a terrifying ordeal.
- An everyday story of everyday folk, but just below this calm surface of normality something horrific is about to take place.
- A horror story with a high-tech setting, perhaps involving the media, computers or the Internet.
- A breakthrough scientific discovery which carries awful consequences.
- A moral slip or compromise which results in a personal or social catastrophe.